T0286857

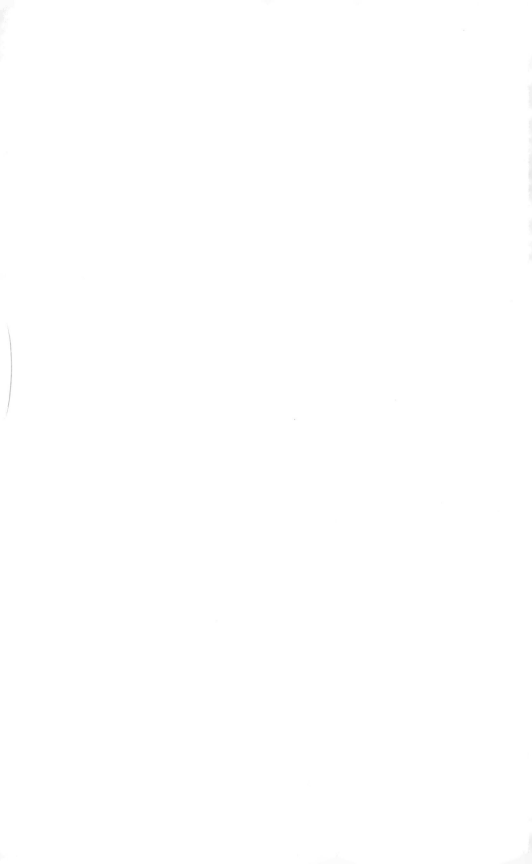

Cambridge Elements ≡

Elements in Histories of Emotions and the Senses
edited by
Jan Plamper
Goldsmiths, University of London

PHANTOM PAINS AND PROSTHETIC NARRATIVES

From George Dedlow to Dante

Alastair Minnis
Yale University, Connecticut

CAMBRIDGE
UNIVERSITY PRESS

University Printing House, Cambridge CB2 8BS, United Kingdom

One Liberty Plaza, 20th Floor, New York, NY 10006, USA

477 Williamstown Road, Port Melbourne, VIC 3207, Australia

314–321, 3rd Floor, Plot 3, Splendor Forum, Jasola District Centre, New Delhi – 110025, India

79 Anson Road, #06–04/06, Singapore 079906

Cambridge University Press is part of the University of Cambridge.

It furthers the University's mission by disseminating knowledge in the pursuit of education, learning, and research at the highest international levels of excellence.

www.cambridge.org
Information on this title: www.cambridge.org/9781108970556
DOI: 10.1017/9781108989695

First published 2021

A catalogue record for this publication is available from the British Library.

ISBN 978-1-108-97055-6 Paperback
ISSN 2632-1068 (online)
ISSN 2632-105X (print)

Phantom Pains and Prosthetic Narratives

From George Dedlow to Dante

Elements in Histories of Emotions and the Senses

DOI: 10.1017/9781108989695
First published online: February 2021

Alastair Minnis
Yale University, Connecticut
Author for correspondence: Alastair Minnis, alastair.minnis@yale.edu

Abstract: 'George Dedlow' is a fictional amputee invented by American Civil War surgeon Weir Mitchell, who coined the phrase 'phantom limb pain' to designate the sensations which seem to emanate from limbs that in reality are missing. Contemporary neuroscience holds that the brain encloses a schema which covers the whole body and asserts its unity, even if certain parts are missing. Reading backwards from Dedlow's sufferings, I trace medieval precedents and parallels, focusing on Augustine and Dante, who subscribed to the notion of a 'body in the soul'. Dante's souls in purgatory self-prosthesize with aerial phantoms as they long for the full embodiment which only the Resurrection can bring. Is a complete body necessary for personhood? And how can the gamut of human feelings be run if parts or indeed the entirety of one's body does not exist? Those issues were as absorbing for medieval thinkers as they are for modern neuroscientists.

Keywords: pain, prosthesis, body schema, Augustine, Dante

ISBNs: 9781108970556 (PB), 9781108989695 (OC)
ISSNs: 2632-1068 (online), 2632-105X (print)

Contents

1 Pain in the Brain

A startling scene unfolded in Leicester Royal Infirmary early in 1995.

> A builder aged 29 came to the accident and emergency department having jumped down on to a 15 cm nail. As the smallest movement of the nail was painful he was sedated with fentanyl and midazolam. The nail was then pulled out from below. When his boot was removed a miraculous cure appeared to have taken place. Despite entering proximal to the steel toecap the nail had penetrated between the toes: the foot was entirely uninjured. (Fisher et al. 1995)

It would seem that the builder's brain had told him he should experience pain, and experience pain he did, even though the body part supposedly affected had not suffered any physical trauma.

'Pain has become one of the most challenging medical mysteries of modern times', remaining 'enigmatic, mysterious, and frustrating' (Boddice 2017, 1–2). It has been studiously avoided (a response now deemed normative), embraced (as in medieval Western Christianity), exploited and monetized (by the modern pharmaceutical industry). Contemporary neuroscientists have freely admitted that it is 'one of the most poorly understood of all sensory experiences'; 'very little is known about [its] physiology' (Ramachandran & Blakeslee 1998, 52; Ramachandran & Hirstein 1998, 1065). What does seem to be the case is that 'pain is not just a message from injured tissues'; there is no simple and 'direct hotline from pain receptors' in the body to 'pain centers' in the brain. And it is abundantly clear that there is 'no pain without brain' (Ingraham 2020). To be more precise, 'The brain does more than detect and analyze inputs; it generates perceptual experience even when no external inputs occur. We do not need a body to feel a body' (Melzack 1992, 126).

That scarcely credible principle, which in relation to the Leicester builder and an abundance of comparable occurrences may even seem laughable, is of exceptional cultural importance. It has been considered, challenged and con-firmed across the centuries in a variety of ways by physicians, philosophers and poets – whatever terminology they may have used in considering the determin-ing, tantalizing, elusive relationship between the *sōma*/body and the *psyche*/soul/mind/brain. The following Element brings together and discusses some of those moments, in a way which reveals their similarities while respecting their singularities. Fundamentally a study in the history of emotions and senses within Western culture, it seeks to harness some of the energy of and synergize some of the varied technical discourses that come from the different critical perspectives of neuroscience, bioethics, medical humanities, literary and cultural criticism, and medieval studies.[1]

The two main protagonists of my narrative are the most intellectually daring of all medieval European poets, Dante Alighieri (d. 1321), and a fictional character, 'George Dedlow', who was created by Silas Weir Mitchell (1829–1914), the 'father' of medical neurology in the United States. A distinguished Civil War physician, Mitchell's intense involvement with amputation surgery and its aftermath inspired him to give 'phantom limb pain' (PLP) the name which has persisted into the twenty-first century and helped drive a substantial literary *oeuvre* which displays a subtle sensibility and remarkable storytelling gifts. An author with a very different sensibility, Owen Wister (1860–1938), who did much to inaugurate the idealizing genre of the cowboy novel, testified to Mitchell's seared conscience by remarking that the experience of treating 'mutilated soldiers' had infused his writing with 'a hideous panorama of the flesh, the mind and the soul' (Herschbach 1995, 187).

The last decades of the twentieth century saw a dramatic reversal in the fortunes of PLP. The celebrity neuroscientist V. S. Ramachandran pronounced it the 'Holy Grail' of neurology and neurobiology: if only a complete vision of PLP could be achieved, its mysteries uncovered, we could peer 'intently and with awe into the cortical processes that are considered constitutive of human experience and the very essence of our humanity' (Crawford 2014, 158–9). What was once a marginal, suspect and often derided syndrome – a mere 'ghost' in the sense of a fantasy or something 'made up' by unreliable witnesses – became of central importance, offered as the skeleton key to understanding human wholeness, our desire for completeness, our sense of personhood.

Amputation and prosthesis, the lack of limbs and the creation of substitutes for them, will feature prominently in the discussion that follows, as I range from missing body parts to missing complete bodies, from what the brain makes of the lack of a limb to what the soul makes of the lack of all the limbs entrusted to it. Does the principle that 'we do not need a body to feel a body' apply even here? Throughout the Middle Ages, that was a matter of intense intellectual debate, with several types of answers in the affirmative being offered, even as the issue of what constituted a body was confronted. Angels and demons, who lacked physical bodies, will make their presences (or, rather, non-presences) felt in this discussion, since theorizing about their occasional embodiment to enable human perception includes some of the best examples of medieval psychosomatic thinking. Discussion of those unfeeling phantoms helped scholars ascertain what it meant to feel distinctly, individually, human.

---

[1] An exemplary illustration of how the history of medicine can synergize with medieval studies has been afforded by the work of Irina Metzler (2006, 2016).

Two sorts of intersection between narrative and prosthesis will be addressed. In the first instance, accounts of literal prosthetic activity (whether by men or angels) will feature prominently, with special attention being paid to Dante's highly original development of the core idea, his description in *Purgatorio* XXV of *ombre*. This is a profound Christianization of the *umbrae* of Virgil's underworld: the shades of the dead, mere shadows, as diaphanous as 'the light breath of a breeze or vanishing dream' (*Aeneid*, VI, 290–4; VI, 700–2). Dante presents his phantoms as eagerly self-prosthesizing, shaping bodies from pliable air, as they long for full embodiment. Beyond that, the metaphorical prospect of a narrative itself enacting prosthesis or refusing to do so will be explored, with reference to Mitchell's uncompromising presentation of the fate of George Dedlow – a tale which offers its reader no consoling scenario of the hero's rehabilitation within 'normal' society.

A major medieval source of psychosomatic thought addressed what happens when the *sōma*/body and the *psyche*/soul/mind/brain are separated by death (a situation sometimes described as being foreshadowed in dreams and other autoscopic, out-of-body experiences, or OBEs). Medieval Western Christianity insisted on the continuous existence of the soul. That was not to be questioned. But how did the lack of its body – a temporary situation, to be sure, for it would return (better than ever) at the General Resurrection – impact on that existence? Another non-negotiable requirement was the occurrence of pleasure in heaven and pain in hell (and purgatory): could phantoms enjoy or suffer without corporeal organs? Here phantom limb pain (and pleasure, for that does exist, according to current neuroscience) takes on a whole new dimension.

My *terminus a quo* consists of writings by Saint Augustine of Hippo in the late fourth century. One of the greatest medieval theologians (arguably *the* greatest in the Western tradition), he devised and deployed an idea of 'body schema' which in certain ways anticipates some of the hypothesizing of contemporary neuroscientists. However, within late-medieval scholasticism, it came under attack; the idea was controversial even then. But before traveling back all that way, I must stop at a few helpful staging posts, to pick up essential conceptual supplies and indicate the high stakes of an inquiry into the pains of phantoms.

First, a fundamental etymology. The term 'psychosomatic', defined by the *Oxford English Dictionary* as 'involving or depending on both the mind and the body', is a compound of the Latin term *psyche* (itself derived from the Greek term *psukhē*), meaning breath, life, mind, soul or spirit, and another Greek term, *sōma*, meaning 'body' (*OED*, s.v. 'psychosomatic'). The compound adjective holds out tantalizing possibilities for the study of what the mind can do when compounded with the body. However, it has become quite toxic among members of the general public (as well as many doctors), who see a diagnosis of psychosomatic illness (or, more commonly, of psychosomatic factors as accentuating an existing bodily illness) as an accusation of malingering, making things up, fakery and lying.

The persistent notion that the body is a sort of machine (which owes a lot to Descartes) means that people expect a material 'fix' for all their ills. Little wonder, then, that the move from organic to psychological diagnosis is so hard to comprehend and so hard to bear for patients presenting with symptoms relating to chest pain, blurred vision, hearing loss, itches and rashes, chronic fatigue and irritable bowel syndrome (to cite examples of illnesses which, in certain cases, have resisted physical explanation). Being told one has a psychological disorder is at times experienced as a humiliation, and patients will go to extraordinary lengths – including having ill-advised surgery – to avoid that slur. All of this has memorably been brought out in a recent popular book by Irish neurologist Suzanne O'Sullivan, which records how she has 'shared' her 'patients' struggle to accept the power of the mind over the body', interacting with people whose lives have been destroyed by 'medical disorders like no others. They obey no rules. They can affect any part of the body' (O'Sullivan 2016, 16, 6). She estimates that 'on an average day perhaps as many as a third of people who go to see their general practitioner have symptoms that are deemed medically unexplained'. Worldwide, the disorders in question 'occur in twenty per cent of patients'. The problem, then, is of massive and global proportions. Humanity is experiencing 'disorders of the imagination restricted only by the limits of the imagination' (7, 6).

2 In Search of Phantoms

No disorder of the imagination has challenged comprehension and strained credibility more than phantom limb syndrome (PLS), whereby patients with a missing limb or some other body part perceive it as being still present, and a source of sensations, particularly pain (PLP) of a kind 'characterized by throbbing, stabbing, electric shock sensations, and even cramped and painfully immobile limb sensations' (Collins et al. 2018, 2168). As George Riddoch (1888–1947) nicely puts it, 'Such a state of affairs was beyond reason and it would not be surprising if the unfortunate patient was regarded as an obstinate, lying fellow or even possessed of the devil. In fact, it was a matter that was better left alone' (Riddock 1941, 197). He expresses surprise concerning the 'frequent refusal of medical men', 'in these days of advanced physiological knowledge', 'to believe that phantom limbs are anything more than psychological abnormalities' (198).[2]

---

[2] Riddoch is credited as being the driving force behind British treatment of spinal injuries during the Second World War.

Riddock's opinion was an exceptionally enlightened one for his time, and the negative attitudes he attributes to contemporary 'medical men' concerning PLP may help us understand why it seems to have been so under-reported in previous times. Today we know that the vast majority of patients experience a vivid phantom almost immediately after the loss of a limb (and in some cases such sensations can persist for many years).[3] The condition must, then, be as old as amputation itself. However, the first viable historical record to have survived from Western Europe is as late as the sixteenth century. It consists of a statement by the innovative French surgeon Ambroise Paré (c. 1510–90), who, living in an age in which firearms were increasingly being used in warfare, had amassed considerable expertise about how gunshot wounds impacted the human body. Paré declared it 'a thing wondrous strange and prodigious, and which will scarce be credited ... that patients, many months after the cutting away of the Leg grievously complained that they yet felt exceeding great pain of that leg so cut off' (Paré 1649, 338).[4]

Can the historical record be traced back even earlier? It has been speculated that medieval accounts of the miraculous restoration of limbs possibly reflect phantom limb phenomena and may be read as imaginary materializations – or perhaps as symbols and metaphors – of them. That is the thesis advanced in a collection of materials published in 1978 by Douglas B. Price and Neil J. Twombly under the title *The Phantom Limb Phenomenon*, which focuses on five miracle stories and records their many variants in an array of original languages. In the following pages, I will discuss the materials and arguments here presented, establishing interpretive contexts in terms of then-prevailing religious doctrines and related social practices, and interspersing a critique of the book's methodology.

Take the case of 'The Leg of Peter of Grenoble', a tale which attained a remarkably wide medieval circulation. Having lost a leg through what seems to have been ergot poisoning (sometimes referred to as *sacer ignis*, 'sacred fire'),[5] the unfortunate Peter gets it back – after a fashion, since in the first instance his limb is not quite what it was. But a second miracle completes the restorative process. In what seems to be the earliest account of these extraordinary events, Guibert of Nogent (1053–1124) recounts how female servants overhear the groans of Peter, who is asleep in bed:

---

[3] Estimates vary considerably (as is unsurprising, given the difficulty of collecting definitive data). Sherman et al. (1984) estimate 78 percent; Ramachandran & Hirstein (1998), between 90 and 98 percent; Nikolajsen & Jensen (2001) put the figure at 60–80 percent.

[4] On early accounts of PLP, see Finger & Hustwit 2003, Wade 2003 and Wade 2009.

[5] A major cause of this disease (which, during the late eleventh and early twelfth centuries, reached epidemic proportions in south-eastern France) was the eating of rye bread made from grain infested with the fungus *claviceps purpurea*. Peter of Grenoble may have suffered from the dry gangrene which a form of this induces.

The cause of these groans was this: in a vision, the Virgin Mother, above all blessed, with Hippolytus the blessed martyr, had stood near his pallet and, as it seemed to him as he lay there, the Virgin Mother gave a command to the martyr, 'Restore him', she said, 'to his original vigor'. Humbly obeying her who gave the command, the martyr picked up the thigh, lower leg, and foot, once scattered in every direction, now by divine intervention consolidated in an instant – in the likeness of the future resurrection – and began to join them to Peter's body, as a slip is joined to a tree. And in this process of engrafting Peter was tortured by such anguish that he in turn showed what he was suffering by gnashing his teeth with loud cries and by repeated snarls and gesticulations of his limbs, so that the aforesaid serving maids . . . were brought running. (Price & Twombly 1978, 11, 16; Migne *PL* 156, 568B–72D)[6]

When a lamp is brought in, the women discover – to their amazement – that Peter has 'two feet and two legs'. Handling the limbs, they perceive that they are real. The master of the house is initially skeptical, believing he is hearing 'mere nursery songs, trifles'. But once he sees, he believes.

Closer examination of the engrafted new limb reveals that it is not a complete replacement:

The new creation was entirely insufficient in strength because of infantile softness and not suitable in size and of a less fitting impressiveness for a young man. The man's limb differed from the old in that there seemed to be present a texture very different from the roughness and coarseness of his other leg . . . The new leg could not, however, in any way be a match for the old leg for supporting the body. (Price & Twombly 1978, 17)

So, for another year, Peter limps along. Then the Virgin and St Hippolytus return, to make considerable improvements:

When, at the kind Virgin's command, the blessed martyr [Hippolytus] had begun to touch the newly molded limb, everything that was lacking in last year's creation except the softness of the skin and the appearance of newness, was shaped to resemble most closely his old leg. Then, Peter, awakening and being thoroughly aware of the truth of the vision through the improvement in his former condition while announcing to all by his bearing the repetition of the supernal miracle, both strengthened belief in the occurrence and also proclaimed that in God and God's works there exists nothing of imperfection.

From this and comparable miracles featuring restored limbs, Price and Twombly conclude that 'the element of sensation or pain in the restored part

---

[6] Throughout I use 'Migne *PL*' to refer to the *Patrologia Latina*, ed. Jacques-Paul Migne, 221 vols (Paris, 1841–65). 'Migne *PG*' refers to its Greek equivalent, the *Patrologia Graeca*, also ed. by Migne, 161 vols (Paris, 1857–66).

either during or after the restoration corresponds basically to the typical aspect of the PL [phantom limb], namely (painful) paresthesias' (Price 1976, 58), i.e. an abnormal sensation, which typically involves feelings of tingling or pricking. Explaining the reasoning behind this, they note that the phantom limb is 'basically a sensory phenomenon' and judge that a reference 'to sensation or pain in the restored part either during or after its restoration more clearly implies the existence' of a phantom limb than 'the more primitive and concrete symbolism involved either in the mere witnessing of the restoration by the amputee in a dream or vision or in the inspection of the restored limb by bystanders in reality'.

Much here can be challenged. First, in the miracle stories in question, it is clear that we are dealing with actual limbs rather than with phantom ones – body parts which, far from existing only in the amputee's mind, are visible to the many people who witness the results of the several miracles. In the case of Peter of Grenoble, Leodegarius, Bishop of Vivers, conducts a thorough investigation to rule out the possibility of this being a mere nursery tale (Price & Twombly 1976, 18). As well as interrogating Peter himself, the Bishop consults people of his diocese that he knows 'to be truthful and men of good lives', requiring them to swear validating oaths and to report publicly, before a substantial audience, what they 'can sincerely say about the sign which is said to have occurred' among them. The sign is visible to all – a regular limb rather than an invisible presence which is felt by a single individual. Far from constituting 'primitive' symbolism which marks the private presence of a phantom limb, 'the inspection of the restored limb by bystanders in reality' marks the public presence of something else: a physical entity, a re-creation of the original limb.

This insistence on reliable and authenticating witnessing of a miracle was quite typical investigative behaviour in the period under discussion. Throughout Western Europe, medieval churchmen regularly carried out extraordinarily detailed and scrupulous investigations to ascertain whether alleged miracles were true or false (Goodich 2007, 69–87, and Bartlett 2013, 333–409). What did or did not happen in the case of the episodes under discussion here is, inevitably, beyond the scope of my analysis. I simply wish to challenge the widespread supposition that medieval people easily and naively believed in miracles. A crucial part of the truth of the miracle involving Peter of Grenoble was that the restored leg was the original one, rather than some sort of fake. Peter invited his inquisitors to look to see if a scar is visible – that would be proof that 'it is going to be the very leg I once had', whereupon the Bishop and his associates searched more closely, and immediately 'found signs of an injury, and did not deny that God is wonderful' (Price & Twombly 1976, 13, 18). Similar evidence is sought and found in the case of the restored nose and lip of a woman called

Gundrada, another victim of ergot poisoning who lived in the Soissons area around 1129. The chronicler Anselm of Gembloux (d. 1136) records that her 'flesh was made like the rest of the flesh, and, what is more wonderful, . . . in the jointure of the old flesh and the new there appeared the sign, as it were, of a very thin thread for a witness' (Price & Twombly 1976, 97; Migne *PL*, 160, 251B-2 C).

The conjunction of old and new flesh is emphasized in several versions of yet another miracle story, that concerning St John of Damascus, who spent most of his life in his monastery near Jerusalem, where he died in 749. According to this improbable yarn, because of a forgery which aroused the anger of the Caliph against John, the hand which allegedly had written the offending document was cut off. Following its restoration, there appeared 'a line marking the cut, God's Mother having arranged this, which showed the amputation to be real' (Price & Twombly 1976, 171; Migne *PG*, 94, 439D-59 C). That statement is from an early, tenth-century version of the story. The point was joyously reiterated during later centuries. Caesarius of Heisterbach (d. c. 1240) assures us that 'it was very nicely restored, a very beautiful scar like a silver thread remaining where the cut had been made' (Price & Twombly 1976, 254–5; Caesarius, ed. Meister 1901, 165–6). Moving forward to the fifteenth century, we find the prolific author and manuscript illuminator Jean Miélot (d. 1472) stating that 'as a sign of the miracle [John] always afterwards had around his arm, there where it was cut off from him, a red cut mark, such as a silk thread' (Price & Twombly 1976, 376–7; *Miracles*, ed. Warner 1885, 40–1).

Should the occasional statement that such amputation marks are beautiful seem surprising, it may be noted that even the glorified bodies of the martyrs, and of Christ himself, were supposed to bear the marks of the terrible physical traumas they once had endured. Thomas Aquinas (d. 1274) declares that such 'scars of wounds' will not be retained 'in so far as they imply a defect, but as signs of the most steadfast virtue' with which they had suffered 'for the sake of justice and faith'. Far from making the glorified bodies of the saints seem deformed, such a sign will be 'a badge of honour, and the beauty of their virtue – a beauty which is in the body, but not of the body – will shine forth in it'. Mechthild of Magdeburg (d. c. 1282/94) went so far as to say that, following Judgment Day, 'the sweet wounds' of Christ 'shall heal, as though a rose petal had been placed on the spot of the wound. One will then see the scars turned bright red – love's color; and they will never fade' (Minnis 2016, 183). In like manner, Peter of Grenoble, Gundrada of Soissons and John of Damascus bear their badges of honour.

The even larger truth served by these accounts is that of the hope and certainty of the General Resurrection, as foreshadowed by Christ's own resurrection. At the end of time, the bodies of men shall arise from the dead, and all their body parts, however dispersed and scattered, shall come together, an extraordinary feat of reconstruction and renewal which 'restoration miracles' were believed to anticipate. This helps explain why all the witnesses and investigators of the events discussed above were so careful in ensuring that the original body parts had indeed been restored. The phrasing in Guibert of Nogent's account of Peter of Grenoble's leg is highly significant: St Hippolytus picks 'up the thigh, lower leg, and foot, once scattered in every direction, now by divine intervention consolidated in an instant – in the likeness of the future resurrection'.

Similar statements are found with regard to the restoration of Gundrada's nose and lip. Hugh Farsit (d. c. 1140), a canon regular of the Abbey of Saint-Jean des Vignes, recounts how the witnesses were 'amazed at the new creation and the pledge of the revivifying resurrection wrought in her deformed nose and lip, and there is joy as though life had returned from the dead' (Price & Twombly 1976, 92, 95; Migne *PL* 179, 1777B-9 C). In 1640, the amputated leg of one Miguel Juan Pellicero was restored and celebrated as 'a most evident proof of our holy Catholic faith because it is truly a proof of the resurrection of the dead, the power of God, the true miracles of the Catholic Church, the powerful intercession of the saints and of the Saint of Saints, Most Holy Mary'.[7] 'On the day of the resurrection, let each one take his own limb', declares the angel Raphael on the occasion of yet another miracle, looking ahead to that glorious future event: the ultimate affirmation of corporeal integrity and the uniqueness of every human body in all its constituent parts (Price & Twombly 1976, 402).[8]

3 False Phantoms

On the one hand, the narratives affirm and certify local re-enactments of the original creation of the world and its first inhabitants. On the other, they are likenesses, pledges and proofs of the re-creation which shall follow the General Resurrection. To serve those purposes, material signs are essential: body parts which can be seen, handled, kissed and revered, along with physical manifestations of the Virgin Mary's power and mercy which may be publicized far and wide, present to be visited and revered by all and sundry. There is nothing 'phantom' about those limbs.

As far as the 'sensation or pain in the restored part' is concerned, it is noteworthy that in the case of 'The Leg of Peter of Grenoble' and comparable miracles the pain occurs either before the loss of the body part (the burning pain

---

[7] As reported by the Spanish Franciscan Antonio Arbiol y Díez (d. 1726). Price & Twombly 1976, 452.

[8] Price and Twombly work from a fifteenth-century of a Greek text, which may well reflect a much earlier tradition.

caused by *sacer ignis* being referenced frequently), during its loss, or in the process of its restoration. St Hippolytus's surgery, the process in which he reassembles Peter's thigh, lower leg, and foot, and rejoins them to their body, is clearly a painful one. That most popular of all late-medieval European collections of saints' lives, the *Legenda aurea* of Jacob of Voragine (d. c. 1298), states that 'during this grafting, Peter felt a pain so great that his cries aroused the whole household' (Price & Twombly 1976, 26). According to the version of Vincent of Beauvais (d. c. 1264), 'in this process of engrafting he was tortured by such burnings that continuing with many shouts, by frequent grimaces and movements he showed what he was suffering' (Price & Twombly 1976, 39). Here the burning pain associated with *sacer ignis* has been transferred to the action whereby the limb is restored.

Indeed, it seems as if the operation on Peter of Grenoble's stump is carried out under a sort of anesthetic, in order to mitigate the terrible pain. For the patient is in a deep sleep. One may compare the most radical instance of surgery recorded in the Bible, when God extracts a rib from Adam's side in order to create Eve, having 'cast a deep sleep upon' the donor (Genesis 2:21). The depth of Peter's sleep is emphasized by the fact that, following the first miracle, he is 'roused with the greatest difficulty' (Price & Twombly 1976, 16). Jean Miélot adds the detail that, even though Peter had 'screamed' in his sleep, he 'was displeased that they had awakened him because of the great pleasure that he was having from his vision', which again indicates the extent to which he had lost consciousness (Price & Twombly 1976, 31). (Peter is also asleep during his follow-up miracle.) Gundrada has her nose and lip restored whilst she is asleep (Price & Twombly 1976, 95, 97, 101, 128, etc.). In some versions of the story of John of Damascus's hand the miracle is described as having occurred while the saint was lying in his bed at night, 'neither sleep nor awake' (Price & Twombly 1976, 177, 183, 186, etc.). Recent research into the phantom limb in dreams has revealed that 'amputees predominantly report having an intact body in their dreams, motivating some researchers to assume an innate body model on which the cognitive processes draw during sleeping' (Bekrater-Bodmann 2016). In medieval restoration miracles, God makes dreams come true, following the innate body model (which is, to apply the medieval belief, of divine design) and rendering the physical body intact. The term 'phantom' can hardly be applied either to the body parts from which the pain initially emanates or to the physical restorations involved in the miracle.

However, in an article published in 1976, Price (also speaking on behalf of Twombly) argues that certain features of Peter of Grenoble's case suggest 'strongly' that Guibert of Nogent 'was describing, not a newly created leg, but an instance of a PL', as is shown by the 'matching' of certain 'elements'. The elements in question are 'insufficient strength', 'softness', 'unsuitable size', 'different texture' and 'inability to support body' (Price 1976, 58). In this and comparable miracles, the restored limbs are often described as being weaker, smaller, of softer texture and even of a different colour than the original healthy limb. Price and Twombly wish to relate such data to modern medical accounts of how patients experience differences between their lost limb and the phantom one, including the intriguing (and well-documented) experience of a phantom arm seeming to become progressively shorter until only the hand remains, a phenomenon now known as 'telescoping' (see, for example, Weiss & Fishman 1963).

I myself find those correspondences neither exact nor convincing. I would say the same of the general appeal that Price and Twombly make to the 'overriding' 'common quality of newness, which represents the newness of change', a 'newness suggested by the deficiencies of the first restoration' (Price 1976, 59). Indeed, they also suggest, here we could be dealing with the representation of 'the change from a painful PL (in the dream, as, probably, in consciousness) to a painless, telescoped PL'. The comparison of the shock and amazement felt by the re-embodied Peter, Gundrada et al. with the change experienced by amputees when they move from awareness of their original limb to awareness of a phantom one, seems far-fetched. Further, if Peter were transitioning from a painful to a pain-free phantom limb, that would be a matter of 'pain in the brain' rather than an external reality visible for all to see. Equally implausible, in my view, is the notion that, in the second restoration, 'the change would be from a telescoped PL to one of normal size and shape, a natural PL' (Price 1976, 59). One moment, a telescoped phantom limb represents a lack of pain; the next, it represents imperfection, a lack which is redressed through the provision of a 'normal'-sized phantom limb. Yet again, we are faced with the fact that the restored limb was visible to many witnesses, including the august and authoritative Bishop of Vivers. The same point can be made about the restored limbs of Gundrada of Soissons and John of Damascus. The optics must be right.

When their attempts to make literal connections come under too much strain, a parallel (and, if necessary, an alternative or indeed over-riding) strategy is brought into play by Price and Twombly: the appeal to metaphor and symbol. Hence, the aforementioned elements of 'insufficient strength', 'softness' and 'inability to support body' may 'of course' (!) 'refer metaphorically to the real insubstantiality of a PL, that is, to the actual inability of a PL to support the body' (Price 1978, 58). The issue of exactly how the metaphors and symbols in question are generated, by which process they develop culturally, is left undiscussed.

At one point Price brings together PLS and an amputee's dream of wholeness as analogous mental experiences, and relates them to the physical completion of a fractured body through the miraculous addition of a missing part. 'The reality of the PL sensations and the reality of the dream of a complete body were so phenomenologically close and in principle so alike as to make the restoration of a lost body part also a reality' (Price 1976, 65–6). Who or what does the 'making' here? (As far as the medieval hagiographers cited above were concerned, of course, the agent was the creator-God, acting on requests from the Virgin Mary. That belief is the driving force behind their narratives.) In this statement of Price's the dream world and the 'real' world confusingly blend: both the dream of a complete body and the thing itself are designated as reality.

But perhaps here we may gain some insight into how myths are made, as envisaged by Price and Twombly. The mechanism implied, though never spelled out, seems to be that medieval people, having acquired knowledge of PL phenomena from amputees, then somehow proceeded to transpose or displace that information onto saints' legends; the wishful thinking of real-life unfortunates, the stuff of their dreams, attained corporeal reality inasmuch as it was inscribed within hagiography. God is credited with having brought about a series of premature resurrections of limbs as a demonstration of his infinite power, manifestations for all to see.

This may be deemed a rather simplistic appropriation of the medieval supernatural as an explanation of narratives which, applying the Price and Twombly method, are to be decoded as evidence of awareness of PLS. 'We believe that the PLP was presented metaphorically and symbolically in folklore long before the first scientific report and description of it appeared in print' (Price 1976, 65). They certainly do and have amassed a remarkable amount of research to support that belief. But we remain far away from the clarity of Ambroise Paré's statement. Peter Halligan's claim that Price and Twombly have 'push[ed] back the recorded history of phantom limb phenomena as far back as the 10th century' is over-optimistic (Halligan 2002, 258).

That said, occasionally something recorded in their anthology stands out and tantalizes. Particularly interesting is a late derivative of the St John of Damascus narrative, in the form of a Middle English homily. Here the pain felt by the victim after the amputation is expressed as follows: 'as he lay in prison, he cried euer to our Lady for helpe, for the ache that he hed on his arme as hit rotede away' (Price & Twombly 1976, 381). The much-earlier, tenth-century version of John's miracle is less specific in this regard (Price & Twombly 1976, 167–71; Migne *PG* 94, 439D-59 C). It has John complaining that his 'pains are becoming intense and they have become unbearable for me'. 'Cure my hand!' he implores the Virgin Mary, declaring that 'the sharpness' of those pains 'will not let up as long' as the cut-off hand hangs high up in the forum: proper burial of his member may abate it. Here, as in the vast majority of limb-restoration miracles, the locus of the pain is insufficiently registered; John could simply have been suffering from pain caused by what nowadays are termed 'scar tissue or neuromas – little curled up clusters or clumps of nerve tissue in the stump' (Ramachandran & Blakeslee 1998, 50). But the Middle English homily seems to specify pain directly caused by the detached member. This could be explained as incomprehension, or an overly free rendering of whatever source was used – or as an addition by someone who was aware of PLP. The latter possibility is, in theory, a quite plausible one; redactors and translators may bring something of their own experience to their rendering of a text, and that is the reason why Price and Twombly collected so many different versions of their five key miracles. But it is hardly definitive.

Another feature of this story is tantalizing also. The early version quoted above seems to indicate a belief that proper burial of a limb can diminish the pain associated with it. Price associates this with folktales recorded in Kentucky and Maryland. Following the amputation of 'a finger, or toe, or an arm', it 'should be buried in a straight position; otherwise the patient will suffer pains from cramp' (Thomas 1920, 93; Price 1976, 62). Further, 'If a member of the body has been amputated and the owner suffers in that member, it is because the amputated part has not been properly buried'. To remedy this situation, 'the member must be dug up and properly buried. Sometimes it is twisted, or a finger or toe is doubled up, and if this is straightened out, the pain ceases'. These bizarre notions may have an explanation in one well-documented aspect of PLP: sometimes it feels as if the phantom limb is paralyzed, locked in a painful position, perhaps the very position it held prior to amputation. To quote one detailed description:

> The bent posture of the lost arm is frequently that which it had for a few hours or days before its removal. There are some cases of hands which have been crushed or burned, and the fingers remained painfully rigid in life or bound in a splint. Just so for ever do they continue when the injured limb has been cut off. (Mitchell 1871, 568)

This phenomenon – regarded nowadays as a stored proprioceptive memory engram of the missing limb, a sort of 'pain memory' retained and continuously acted on by the brain[9] – may have given rise to the belief that, if a missing limb is buried properly, the pain associated with it shall disappear.[10]

---

[9] Flor (2002, 877) has emphasized that 'pain memories established prior to the amputation are powerful elicitors of phantom limb pain'. See also Collins et al. 2018, 2171; Katz & Melzack 1990; Ramachandran & Blakeslee 1998, 51–6.

[10] Ramachandran has, less drastically, sometimes achieved the same end by his 'mirror box' therapy. On some occasions, PLP can be relieved when a mirror reflects an amputee's remaining limb, giving the impression that both limbs are present. An illusion that the missing limb is moving easily is thereby created, so the phantom can be unclenched, attaining a comfortable

Another (at least partial) explanation is available: the long-standing resistance of the Christian Church (particularly the Catholic Church) to cremation of the body, which can extend to an abhorrence of disposing of body parts by means other than internment. Cremation was long seen as a pagan ritual (literally in use among the pagans with whom the early Christians contended) and a practice which 'shamelessly ridiculed the doctrine of the resurrection of the body' (Prothero 2003, 74; see further Laqueur 2015, 495–548). At the General Resurrection, our fractured body parts shall (somehow) reunite, so in the meantime they must be treated with all due respect, and certainly not burned. What was billed as the first cremation in modern America did not take place until 1876.[11] More conservative attitudes may be reflected in folklore; hence the insistence on proper burial for detached limbs. Here, then, is an intriguing mixture of science and demotic belief. But we cannot infer from this that St John of Damascus sought to stop his phantom limb pain, by acting on the belief that if he should bury his severed hand 'beneath the earth … the great pain may abate' (Price & Twombly 1976, 171). In medieval Europe, our phantoms remain elusive.

We are on more secure ground when tracing the origin of the phrase 'phantom limbs'. It was first used in an article published in 1871 by the American Civil War physician Silas Weir Mitchell: the same article I have just quoted on how certain postures of limbs can continue to cause distress even if the limbs themselves are absent. What did the word 'phantom' mean to Mitchell? Thanks to the resources of the *Oxford English Dictionary*, we can get a clear idea. A primary sense was of 'a thing (usually with human form) that appears to the sight or other sense, but has no material substance; an apparition, a spectre, a ghost' (*OED* s.v. *phantom*, n. and adj., 2 a). For instance, writing of the slaughter at the Battle of Culloden (1746), Tobias Smollett spoke of how 'The pale phantoms of the slain / Glide nightly o'er the silent plain', and an 1843 entry cites the prolific American philosopher and poet Ralph Waldo Emerson writing contemptuously of 'how easy it is to demonstrate to show' an unenlightened materialist 'that he also is a phantom walking and working amid phantoms'. (A characteristic remark:

position. Ramachandran & Blakeslee 1998, 46–9. Herta Flor accepts that this therapy works in some cases (Flor et al. 2006, 879). Not everyone has been convinced. Aternali & Katz 2019 declare robustly that 'the results of the most recent studies evaluating the efficacy of MT [mirror therapy] for PLP are not promising. Overall, MT does not appear to reduce PLP to a greater degree than control or other known treatments'. In a personal communication, Tamar Makin has suggested that 'mirror box treatment is no better than snake oil' – a colloquial analogy with special resonance for neuroscientists, given that Weir Mitchell was an expert on snake venom, and ridiculed the excessive claims of snake oil salesmen.

[11] The corpse being that of an Austrian nobleman, Baron Le Palm, and the event being managed by members of the Theosophical Society (Prothero 2003, 15–45). Turning to Britain, the so-called Cremation Act was passed by Parliament in 1902, legalizing the burning of human remains and enabling the establishment of crematoria.

Emerson was a leader of the 'transcendentalist movement', which sought to transcend the purely material world of reason, whilst not necessarily being opposed to the empiricism of science.) Also current were the meanings of 'something merely imagined; an image in a dream, vision, etc.' and a '(usually delusory) notion or idea which plays on the mind or haunts the imagination' – well illustrated by Joseph Addison's 1706 exclamation, 'Farewel sorrow, farewel fear, / They're fantoms all!' (*phantom*, n. and adj., 3 a).

All of these meanings have a long history. Looking at the early uses of 'phantom' (which derives from the Latin *phantasma*; cf. Medieval French *fantosme*), three strands of meaning are evident: a spectre or apparition; an illusion or deception; and a mental image, a product of the imagination – including something 'imaginary' in the negative sense of 'something made up', a fiction. This understanding of phantasms as mysterious things of the mind which are not materially 'real' and may be deceptive, was reinforced by the meaning of the possible English synonym 'ghost', which designated a spiritual being, whether demon or angel, the soul of a dead person or indeed the soul in general as opposed to the body (*DMLBS* s.v. *phantasma*).

Here, then, is the semantic legacy, the cultural baggage, which the term 'phantom' brought with it, and of which Mitchell was very aware. His choice of the term as applied to a strange and disturbing neurological condition, acceptance of which could provoke accusations of credulousness or deception, was quite deliberate, chosen in preference to some more bland, uncontentious and ostentatiously scientific term. The discourse of ghosts, illusions and hauntings features prominently in his attempts to come to grips with a phenomenon that pushed at the boundaries of what, in his day, was accepted – and acceptable – medical knowledge. And Mitchell's first venture into that mysterious world, a short narrative entitled *The Case of George Dedlow* threatened to develop (or deteriorate?) into a ghost story.

4 *The Case of George Dedlow*: Phantom Limbs and Resistance to Prosthetic Narrative

Mitchell produced a substantial corpus of poems and novels – thereby displaying a talent of considerable usefulness in his depiction of startling illnesses. He 'saw hundreds of mangled bodies in excruciating shock and pain –a raw and fierce corporeality that created unique clinical opportunities' (Cervetti 2012, 87).[12] And also, it may be added, unique opportunities for the creation of

---

[12] Cervetti's biography is troubled by its author's belief that her misogynistic subject waged a 'war against women' (2), not least in his promotion of a 'rest cure' as a means of treating hysteria (a practice which endured as long as Virginia Woolf's time, when it was imposed upon her). This

graphic narrative which draws on that grisly first-hand experience. His 1871 article (published in the popular *Atlantic Monthly*) movingly describes how an amputee can be 'haunted, as it were, by a constant or inconstant fractional phantom of so much of himself as has been lopped away – an unseen ghost of the lost part' (Mitchell 1871, 565). A disturbing phantasmagoria is presented of a legion of 'spirit limbs' troubling the memories of many fine men.

> There is something almost tragical, something ghastly, in the notion of these thousands of spirit limbs haunting so many good soldiers, and every now and again tormenting them with the disappointments which arise when, the memory being off guard for the moment, the keen sense of the limb's presence betrays the man into some effort, the failure of which of a sudden reminds him of his loss. (Mitchell 1871, 564–6)

Note the careful affirmation of the masculinity of these 'good soldiers'; they have not been unmanned by their traumatizing experiences but rather suffer them bravely.[13] This is explicable by the fact that Civil War soldiers who had lost limbs (and, indeed, many who had not) were sometimes diagnosed as being 'hysterical'. Hysteria had been regarded as an inherently feminine disorder, the result of a wandering and troublesome womb. But the abundance of evidence from Civil War case histories held out the possibility of a major rethink, with hysteria becoming 'a disease of the nervous system, impartial to sex and requiring neither emasculation nor a faulty uterus to thrive' (Cervetti 2012, 83).[14] A feature of that rethink was the recognition of 'phantom limb pain' as a viable neurological condition.

Mitchell was on the front line both literally and metaphorically but, fearing ridicule, initially was hesitant about issuing his findings in a professional

---

treatment, as Cervetti says, 'was born out of the extended period of rest necessary to allow the soldier's body to repair damaged nerve tissue' (84).

[13] Later in his article, Mitchell, having given an account of an amputee who received electric shock treatment which revived sensations in the fingers and thumb of a lost hand, exclaims, 'To become thus again conscious of a ghostly bit of yourself which had been laid for years must certainly be somewhat surprising to the least emotional of men' (568). Manly emotions are in no way compromised here – a matter of paramount importance, given then-prevailing medical, and social, values. In his book on nerve injuries, Mitchell remarks that phantom pain reduced even the 'strongest man' to being 'scarcely less nervous than the most hysterical girl' (Mitchell 1872, 196). Erin O'Connor has written brilliantly of how 'Victorian ideals of health, particularly of male health, centered upon the concept of physical wholeness: A strong, vigorous body was a primary signifier of manliness'. Dismemberment 'unmanned' amputees, 'producing neuro-logical disorders that gave the fragmented male body – or parts of it anyway – a distinctly feminine side'. 'An incomplete man was not a true one', and thus diminished, a man could take on feelings supposedly appropriate to a woman, running the risk of succumbing to effeminizing hysteria (O'Connor 1997, 744–7).

[14] The scholarship on hysteria (subsequently termed 'conversion disorder') is very extensive. Suffice it to recommend here a recent neuroscientific 'history', in the first section of Hallett, Stone & Carson (2016, 3–44).

medical journal. So he turned to fiction – publishing in 1866 the grotesque tale of one George Dedlow, a Civil War company commander who was 'stripped of every limb' (Mitchell 1900, 130), both legs and both arms having been amputated. Here is the powerful scene in which Dedlow discovers he has lost his second leg – though continuing to experience sensations which, he believes, issue from it and prove its existence.

> I . . . was suddenly aware of a sharp cramp in my left leg. I tried to get at it to rub it with my single arm [which he will lose later!], but, finding myself too weak, hailed an attendant. 'Just rub my left calf', said I, 'if you please'.
>
>> 'Calf?' said he. 'You ain't none. It's took off'.
>> 'I know better', said I. 'I have pain in both legs'.
>> 'Wall, I never!' Said he. 'You ain't got nary leg'.
>
> As I did not believe him, he threw off the covers, and, to my horror, showed me that I had suffered amputation of both thighs, very high up. (128)

Given his own medical knowledge – Dedlow was training as a physician before being obliged to enlist – he brings a scientific curiosity to bear in conversing with other wounded men who are enduring similar sufferings.

> I found that the great mass of men who had undergone amputations for many months felt the usual consciousness that they still had the lost limb. It itched or pained, or was cramped, but never felt hot or cold. If they had painful sensations referred to it, the conviction of its existence continued unaltered for long periods; but where no pain was felt in it, then, by degrees the sense of having that limb faded away entirely. (131)

Here, then, are the classic symptoms of 'phantom limb pain' – described in language which, within North American and Western European medicine, has stood the test of time. As Cervetti has said, 'Through his own words as physician and artist', Mitchell 'attempted to construct a language that communicated' the devastating, and scarcely credible, 'effects of this type of nerve injury'. Indeed, in this sphere 'he seems driven to make and remake language' (Cervetti 2012, 77, 82). That language has endured, the term 'phantom limb pain' has persisted, even though the science surrounding it has changed considerably.

But, back in the late 1860s, Mitchell was worried that *The Case of George Dedlow* might have been a fiction too far. In his 1871 article, he does not claim the story as his own, instead referring to an unidentified author who had 'tak[en] advantage of the freedoms accorded to a writer of fiction' to describe 'certain psychological states' characteristic of amputees which are 'so astounding in their character that he certainly could not have conceived it possible that his humorous sketch, with its absurd conclusion, would for a moment mislead anyone' (Mitchell

1871, 564). The first part of that statement is quite disingenuous, though under-standable given Mitchell's concerns about his professional reputation. The tragedy of George Dedlow was well received by a sympathetic public that assumed the protagonist was a real-life human being – and, indeed, it had empowered actual amputees to come forward with accounts of their own phantom limbs. In light of that response, it is difficult to see how the tale could have 'mislead anyone'. But that 'absurd conclusion' – to which we may now turn – is more problematic.

George Dedlow meets a wounded sergeant who claims to converse 'daily with the great and the good who have left this here world' (Mitchell 1871, 141). Intrigued, Dedlow attends a séance himself, at which certain spirits, by knock-ing, spell out the names of departed loved ones. The medium 'Sister Euphemia' undertakes to summon to their circle whatever spirit he may bring to mind (Mitchell 1900, 146–8). She senses the presence of two spirits. Numbers are duly tapped out: 3486 and 3487. The medium is puzzled – but Dedlow instantly recognizes them as the numbers given to his two amputated legs by the United States Army Medical Museum in which they now repose. 'They are my legs – my legs!' A phantasmagoric episode follows in which Dedlow imagines them as reattached to his stumps – whereupon, for a few seconds, he seems able to walk. A cruel pseudo-resurrection of his lower limbs is experienced:

> Suddenly I felt a strange return of my self-consciousness. I was reindividua-lized, so to speak. A strange wonder filled me, and, to the amazement of every one, I arose. And, staggering a little, walked across the room on limbs invisible to them or me. It was no wonder I staggered, for, as I briefly reflected, my legs had been nine months in the strongest alcohol. At this moment all my new friends crowded around me in astonishment. Presently, however, I felt myself sinking slowly. My legs were going, and in a moment I was resting feebly on my two stumps upon the floor. It was too much. All that was left of me fainted and rolled over senseless. (148)[15]

The performances of mediums were abhorred by Mitchell as a form of quackery – as is made utterly clear by his *The Autobiography of a Quack*, a narrative which came to be published as a companion piece to *The Case of George Dedlow*. So why then did he chose to end the earlier story with an episode which, given the

---

[15] A powerful real-life parallel to this episode involves a subject described by Brugger (2008, 1275) as having recalled a startling dream 'in which she had an intact body (she had been born without forearms and legs). In that dream, a nightmare in fact, she visited a church in the ominous city of Lourdes and felt that arms and legs grew out of her stumps; she felt most horrified by this experience'. This, Professor Brugger tells me (personal communication), was the woman referred to as 'A.Z.' in Brugger 2006, 183–4; Brugger, Kollias et al. 2000; and Funk, Shiffrar & Brugger 2005. 'Her parents (I think that originally she grew up in a Catholic environment) wanted her to wear prostheses, but she very vehemently refused to carry them because she wanted to show the world how strong one could be without having limbs.'

author's own attitudes, seems destined to undermine the account of phantom limbs which had come before, phantoms of a very different level of credibility than the ones summoned up by Sister Euphemia and her kind? It was one thing to test the reactions of his readers to symptoms of a neurological condition for which he had an abundance of case histories, but to associate those facts with the fakery of séances seems a strange move to make, given the obvious risk of devaluing the former by association with the latter. Did his instincts as a teller of tales take over here, with the symmetry of two types of 'ghost' having proved appealing? Whatever the motivation, the episode is dominated by the dreadful moment when Dedlow realizes he has no limbs to support him, that his losses are permanent and will challenge his very sense of being.

The postbellum years saw a rapid growth in prosthetic technology, with ingenious devices of metal, wood and leather being invented to replicate the functions of limbs and, in some cases, to mimic their appearance (Herschbach 1997). 'Prosthesis' will be a crucial term in the following discussion. Foundationally, it shall be used to describe 'the replacement of defective or absent parts of the body by artificial substitutes' (*OED* s.v. *prosthesis*, n., 2a).[16] This is a medical usage, which came into vogue in the early eighteenth century, following a much earlier grammatical usage, which denoted the addition of a letter or syllable, usually at the beginning of a word (cf. the post-classical Latin term *prosthesis,* derived from the ancient Greek πρόσθεσις, meaning 'addition'; *OED* s.v. *prosthesis*, n., 1). By a process of addition and replacement, nineteenth-century technicians and surgeons sought to render amputees able-bodied, to enable them to look like, and feel like, whole men again, prepared to resume their labours. Lacking such intervention, the wretched Dedlow, reduced to a mere torso, laments his incompleteness. 'At times the conviction of my want of being myself was overwhelming and most painful', he declares. 'It was, as well as I can describe it, a deficiency in the egoistic sentiment of individuality' (Mitchell 1900, 138).

That attitude consolidates the claim of *The Case of George Dedlow* to be considered in relation to 'prosthesis narrative', a textual mode of considerable importance for the history of emotions and the senses. Something of Mitchell's achievement may be conveyed by drawing on the discourse offered in David Mitchell and Sharon Snyder's essay collection, *Narrative Prosthesis*. The narrative of George Dedlow powerfully questions 'the relationship between constructed and material identities' (Mitchell & Snyder 2014, 3).[17] It combines

---

[16] The term is also used (sense 2b) to designate the actual object of prosthesis, an artificial replacement for a part of the body. That sense also goes back to the early eighteenth century.

[17] *The Case of George Dedlow* is absent from this book, in which it obviously belongs, but, of course, no single collection could cover the vast range of relevant materials. Within the sphere of literary theorizing, a highly ambitious contribution has recently been made by Boxall 2020. As

an expression of that 'noncompliance with social expectations about valid physical and cognitive lives' which is characteristic of disability, with what Mitchell himself described (deploying self-protective dismissiveness) as 'the freedom accorded to a writer of fiction' (Mitchell 1871, 564). In particular, Mitchell refuses to engage in 'the quick repair of disability' current in so many 'mainstream representations' (Mitchell & Snyder 2014, 9). That is to say, in much writing featuring disabled people some form of narrative supplement – going beyond the mere addition of a letter or syllable, to hark back to the ancient grammatical sense of prosthesis – offers a form of consolation to able-bodied readers, a feel-good factor which renders the narrative acceptable. The 'minimal goal' of prosthesis is, through addition and replacement, 'to return one to an acceptable degree of difference'. But Dedlow's uncompromising disability refuses 'its desired cultural return to the land of the normative' (Mitchell & Snyder 2014, 7, 9).

Such resistance to narrative prosthesis is writ large in the story's ending, which denies the reader any comfort: 'I have so little surety in being myself that I doubt my honesty in drawing my own pension, and feel absolved from gratitude to those who are kind to a being who is uncertain of being enough himself to be conscientiously responsible' (Mitchell 1900, 148–9). How can a non-person draw a pension? How can someone who is insufficiently himself, a mere 'fraction of a man', possess the amount of moral scrupulosity needed to express gratitude, thereby accepting normal – and normalizing – standards of behaviour? A major behavioural prosthesis, so to speak, is needed for George Dedlow to function in society; to be welcome therein entails presenting a degree of difference which is acceptable. Neither more nor less than that.

Dedlow's confrontation of the 'deficiency' in 'the egoistic sentiment of [his] individuality', the fractionalization of his identity as a man, should not be mistaken for some (routine, predictable) form of misanthropy; to do that would trivialize his musings, and bring them within the comfort zone of a wider audience. The depth of that confrontation profoundly resists the self-prosthesizing that a return to his socially-appropriate community would require. Rather he concludes, without self-pity, that 'a man is not his brain, or any one part of it, but all of his economy, and that to lose any part must lessen this sense of his own existence' (Mitchell 1900, 139). On the one hand, this vision of wholeness seems to affirm the integrity of the body in all

---

a counterpoint to *mimesis*, the imitation of external reality thought of as material (so well discussed by Erich Auerbach), he opposes *prosthesis*, involving responsiveness to the prosthetic augmentations with which our given bodies extend into the world, creating reality as much as (or, in some instances, more than) imitating pre-existing stable forms.

its parts. Each part matters and is a vital member of that total economy which constitutes an individual; its loss is of great consequence, lessening a person's sense of their existence in its entirety. So, then, a man may not be reduced to his brain (or mind or psyche). Here Mitchell's powerful empathy with the numerous wounded soldiers he cared for shines through. On the other hand, Dedlow's vision of wholeness comprises the integrity of the body and the brain as a composite, fully integrated, entity. Here is a definite adumbration of the contemporary neuroscientific belief that there is 'no pain without brain', sensation being produced through an interrelation of brain and body.

It may be presumed that Mitchell's secularizing impulses as a medical man drove the refusal in his narrative of any 'quick repair of disability', including the appeal to religion. And yet: the latter part of *The Case of George Dedlow* seems to allow for the existence of something above and beyond, which transcends the reaches of any ridiculous medium.

> Betwixt two worlds I drift,
> A bodiless soul again,
> Between the still thoughts of God
> And those which belong to men ...
> ('Night – Lake Helen'; Mitchell 1883, 69–70)

Those words come from one of Mitchell's evening meditations, as described in his 'Camp Fire Lyrics' sequence of poems. It bespeaks an awareness of the transcendent thoughts of God which was shared by his character George Dedlow: 'I am eager for the day when I shall rejoin the lost members of my corporeal family in another and a happier world' (Mitchell 1900, 149). Might Mitchell have found in his cases of PLP some intimations of immortality, which he sought to mask, and protect himself from possible ridicule, by associating those same experiences with the fakery of mediums, for which he had no respect whatever – and see how his readers would react? As a boy, he had been required to read a Bible text daily and to attend church regularly (his mother was a devout Presbyterian), and though as a young man he had pronounced that indoctrination boring, in later life he came to place his hope in 'the promise of another earth that shall unriddle by and bye the many things that are dark today' (qtd. by Cervetti 2012, 100, 231).

There is a crucial historical context here. In the second half of the nineteenth century, American discussions about phantom limbs were closely linked to explorations of the supernatural within spiritualism, which aimed to enable manifestations of lost bodies through séances of the kind parodied in *The Case of George Dedlow* (see especially Satz 2010 and, more generally, Oppenheim

1985). Long after the medical profession definitively dismissed such associ-ations as quaint things of the past, it continued to consider phantom limbs as clinical curiosities, thereby fostering neglect of this fascinating phenomenon until the late twentieth century. As Katja Guenther says, 'It is telling that the term "phantom" stuck. The syndrome and the pain associated with it remained difficult to reconcile with mainstream medicine' (Guenther 2016, 343). It was an appropriate term for a disturbing spectral syndrome that evaded the down-to-earth definitions of medical science. 'Like a ghost it was hard to prove, pin down, or analyse, perhaps even believe' (343).

5 Phantom Pain and 'Bodies in the Brain'

In our own time, the search for such phantoms has attained a high level of scientific respectability. The wide extent of PLP has been acknowledged even as recent wars have produced large numbers of amputees; as of January 1, 2018, in Iraq or Afghanistan some 1,718 US military service members had lost at least one major limb (Perry et al. 2018). PLP is now understood as a global phenomenon, which cuts across boundaries of nation, region, ethnicity, class, gender and age. In a short monograph, justice cannot possibly be done to the research of the many neurologists, psychotherapists, psychologists and cognitive behaviour therapists who have contributed to this revolution in thinking, many of their names scarcely known beyond their professional specialisms.

V. S. Ramachandran (b. 1951) is particularly well-known, given his widely read popularizing work; in 2011 *Time* magazine listed him as one of the one hundred most influential people in the world. He has eloquently promoted the idea that, far from phantom limbs being peripheral or indeed freakish, they shed light on neurological processes central to *all* mental activity. Here we may be seeing 'a new route to the Holy Grail of neurobiology', Ramachandran has been quoted as saying; 'the exotic phenomenon of phantom limb' prob-ably offers 'one keenly magnified perspective on what routinely happens in the brain as we engage the world around us' (Crawford 2014, 158). In order to communicate something of the excitement (and indeed the hype) surrounding such research, Cassandra Crawford has opined that it positions phantoms as 'the Holy Grail of neurobiology, sacred objects with wondrous and enigmatic qualities'; here are 'unique neurologic windows that allow us to peer intently and with awe into the cortical processes that are considered constitutive of human experience and the very essence of our humanity' (159). (The fifth chapter of Crawford's biopolitical study is entitled 'Phantoms in the Brain: The Holy Grail of Neuroscience'.)

If one can speak of a Holy Grail of this kind, then Ramachandran is definitely prominent in its quest, although his enthusiasm has led him to make 'sometimes bold and sweeping' conclusions, and offer 'vague' answers to large questions about the uniqueness of the human species. I draw those phrases from remarks by Peter Brugger (Brugger 2012). (For Ramachandran's patronizing response, see Ramachandran 2012.) Another major grail knight was the Canadian psychologist Ronald Melzack (1929–2019), renowned for his revolutionary 'gate control' theory of pain (non-painful sensations can override and reduce painful ones), and his development of the McGill University Pain Questionnaire, a self-reporting scale of classifying and rating pain which has exerted enormous influence, having been translated into some twenty-six languages (though on occasion the translation moves some distance away from the original; Boddice 2017, 42). Melzack (1989, 9) has extolled the high stakes of the grail quest by claiming the brain is capable of creating sensation to such an extent that, despite 'the absence of inputs from the body, virtually every quality of sensation and affect is experienced, from excruciating pain to orgasm'.

Back to the sad and sombre words of the subject's founding father in America. In an 1871 article, Mitchell suggests that 'the form of neuralgic torture to which stumps are liable arises from inflamed or hardened conditions of the divided nerves' (Mitchell 1871, 565). 'The ends of the nerves undergo a curious alteration', declares the fictional but verisimilar George Dedlow, 'and get to be enlarged and altered', consequently occasioning 'a more or less constant irritation of the nerve fibers'. 'The pain keeps the brain ever mindful of the missing part, and, imperfectly at least, preserves to the man a consciousness of possessing that which he has not' (Mitchell 1900, 132–3). To rephrase that in contemporary neuroscientific language, 'the frayed and curled-up nerve endings in the stump (neuromas) that originally supplied the hand tend to become and inflamed and irritated, thereby fooling higher brain centers into thinking that the missing limb is still there' (Ramachandran & Blakeslee, 1998, 23). However, in the view of contemporary neuroscientists in general, while tumours formed on a nerve cell sheath can contribute to phantom sensations, they are merely part of a much more complicated picture – as is evidenced by the fact that phantoms are experienced by patients born without limbs (i.e. limb aplasia, a phenomenon recently addressed by Brugger et al. 2000; Funk, Shiffrar & Brugger 2005; and Brugger & Funk 2007).

Answers have been sought in the somatosensory cortex, that 'great convoluted mantle on the surface of the brain' (Ramachandran & Blakeslee 1998, 25) on which the entire body, with all its constituent parts, seems to be mapped. Every point on the body's surface has a corresponding point in the brain; indeed, one may speak of a 'body in the brain'. The cortex maintains a body representation which remains with its owner perpetually. In the case of PLP, this representation keeps on insisting that a limb exists even when it does not, the brain experiencing sensations which apparently emanate from that limb – sensations which can take the form of acute pain.

Those statements, while useful, simplify a richly complicated state of affairs. 'The brain contains multiple representations of the body' (Haggard & Wolpert 2005), according to a current neuroscientific consensus; therefore one may speak, with greater precision, of 'bodies' (definitely in the plural) 'in the brain'. In the first instance, we may acknowledge the existence of the 'little man in the brain' named a 'homunculus' by the Canadian neurosurgeon Wilder Penfield (1891–1976) in his description of the process whereby sensory input fields project to maps of the body surface, and body segments, in the primary somatosensory cortex. These maps reflect the distribution of sensory receptors within the body, which does not correspond to the actual body shape, surface and dimensions that we see when looking at ourselves in a mirror. The relative density of cutaneous tactile receptors on our several body parts is disproportionate to that; different body parts experience very different degrees of sensitivity of tactile stimulation. Hence, in the now-famous 1950 artist's impression of the 'Penfield Map' (Penfield & Rasmussen 1950),[18] the hands and lips are grotesquely enlarged, occupying as much space as the body's entire trunk; indeed, the hands look like two large clubs which drag the body forward, scraping the ground like the action of some looming orangutan.

This is far from the noble *imago Dei* in which the first human was created, according to generations of Christian theologians who celebrated the pristine beauty and perfect proportions of Adam in their amplification of the creation narrative in the Book of Genesis. Aquinas imagines the father of humankind standing proudly erect in his stately aspect, his head raised aloft, in contrast with the irrational lower animals whose faces are positioned close to the ground, so they can seek out food (Minnis 2016, 28–9). The Latin term *homunculus* itself goes far back beyond the Middle Ages, being recorded in Cicero and Plautus as designating a little or a weakly man (Glare 2012, s.v. *homunculus*, i. 879). In Medieval Latin it carried the sense of a mere man, a poor creature or a worthless fellow – a miserable sinner deserving of divine punishment (*DMLBS*, s.v. *homunculus*). A widely-used grammar-school text, the *Parabolae* attributed to Alan of Lille (d. 1202/3), contains the bracing statement that the greedy man who would not be content with 'booty from all lands, or glory, or riches, or honor', quite appropriately ends up with nothing. 'It is only justice that the pathetic man (*homunculus*) who wants sole possession of the earth, should have absolutely no

---

[18] For a cogent account and critique, see Schott 1993.

part of it' (iii,16; tr. Thomson & Perraud, 307). The miniscule significance of the *homunculus* is brought out well in St Augustine's statement that, because God can comprehend an infinite number of things, and comprehends all that is incomprehensible, 'who are we mere men (*homunculi*), that we should presume to set limits to his knowledge?' In the sixteenth century, the homunculus became a manikin with great powers, supposedly produced by alchemists (transitioning from making gold to making life) in a grisly parody of the divine creation. Whence it passed into fictional literature concerned with the search for artificial intelligence, Frankenstein's monster being one spectacular derivation (Newman 1999; Newman 2004, 164–237). Such negative, even sinister, associations may have been in Penfield's mind when he named his monster, a distorted image of the human form yet a true representation of cortical reality rather than the stuff of nightmares.

However, this is not the only alleged 'body in the brain'. The primary sensory input handled by the cortical homunculus is further processed, to construct higher-order, more cognitive representations of the body. At the cognitive level, a crucial distinction has been made between two (at least two) different higher-order body representations, the 'body schema' and the 'body image'. This terminology goes back to a foundational study by the English neurologist Sir Henry Head (1861–1940)[19] together with his Irish colleague Sir Gordon Holmes (1876–1965). By 'body image' they understood a conscious visual representation of the way the body appears to the human gaze, the way in which the brain internally images how the body looks externally.[20] But that was not their main concern. What they, and Walter Russell Brain (1895–1996) after them, really prioritized was the 'schema'[21] that relates to body posture or passive movement, the brain's 'power of projecting our recognition of posture, movement and locality beyond the limits of our own bodies' (Head & Holmes 1911–12, 187–8; Head 1918; Brain 1941). Indeed, they remark rather whimsically, 'a woman's power of localization may extend to the feather in her hat'. To draw on a later cogent summary of the theory, the body schema is 'a central representation of the body's spatial properties, that includes the length of limb segments, their hierarchical arrangement, the configuration of the segments in space and the shape of the body surface' (Haggard & Wolpert 2005).

---

[19] The imaginative Henry Head was, inter alia, a minor poet and a lover of literature, who became firm friends with Thomas Hardy and Siegfried Sassoon. He features in Pat Barker's Booker Prize-nominated novel *Regeneration* (1991), in respect of his work with psychiatrist William Rivers on nerve regeneration.

[20] This is what Paillard 1999, in his elaboration of Head and Holmes's comments, called 'an internal representation in the conscious experience of visual, tactile and motor information of corporal origin' (197), that being how they understood 'body image'.

[21] Brain 1941 speaks of the 'body scheme' and 'body pattern'.

As Macdonald Critchley (1979) has memorably remarked, Head and Holmes's article opened a 'Pandora's box which let loose a spate of metaphysics, much of it sheer verbiage'.

> Terminology blossomed so that terms like 'body image', 'body schema', 'corporeal schema', '*image de soi*' were employed more or less interchangeably. It soon became obvious that thinking was becoming so muddled that the various expressions were made to stand in the literature for different ideas at different times by different writers. At one moment the idea was perceptual; at another it was a conceptual one. Part of the trouble was due to a lack of clear definition, the one put forward by Head and Holmes being more elucidatory than hermeneutic.... Clearly an all-embracing term is needed, one which combines conceptual with the more tangible perceptual components. (Critchley 1979, 93)

Neuroscientists have been making similar complaints ever since.[22] No all-embracing term has turned up, probably because none can exist.

'We allow ourselves to speak of the body image and other such *scheme* or ghosts, which, I think, we would well be rid of by adopting a method of intellectual exorcism' (Spicker 1975, 182). That was the robust proposal of Stuart F. Spicker (1937–2013), a pioneer in the field of medical ethics, here advocating the expulsion of the phantoms created by confused and confusing terminology. Responding to that statement, de Vignemont 2010 claims that it goes too far. 'It is one thing to get rid of the confusion in the literature; it is another thing to get rid of the notions of the body schema and the body image themselves with no further argument' (669). Just because it is a 'slippery issue' does not mean we should let it fall from our grasp. 'Body representations are not ghosts', de Vignemont continues; 'every single morning, they allow us to comb our hair, to grasp our cup of tea, and to enjoy the warm feeling of the sun on our skin'. Or, it may be added, to detect how far the feather in one's hat extends in space. Given the important role those representations play in our lives, which we quickly realize when they are disturbed, any talk of exorcism in the sense of rejection and banishment seems inappropriate. 'So yes, we should adopt a method of intellectual exorcism, but only to clarify the conceptual landscape of the study of body representations'.

The study of body representations has indeed been clarified and in great detail. Bodies in the brain have multiplied, and the terminology continues to proliferate, in the (vain?) attempt to achieve that hermeneutic precision for which Critchley appealed. So, we have had treatments of, for example, the 'self-

---

[22] A few examples, among many, include Paillard 1975 and Paillard 1999; several essays in Berlucchi & Aglioti 2010; De Preester & Knockaert 2005. Stamenov 2005 does a remarkable job of establishing a grounding interface between 'body schema' and 'body image', examining how the activation of the former may lead to experience of the latter.

model' (Metzinger 2000; Metzinger 2004); the 'superficial schema' (Mancine, Longo, Iannetti & Haggard, 2001; Coslet & Lie, 2004); the 'body structural description' (Buxbaum & Coslett, 2001; Corradi-Dell'Acqua et al. 2008); 'body semantics' (Coslett, Saffram & Schwoebel 2002; also Kemmerer & Tranel 2008); and the 'body model' (Longo & Haggard 2010; Longo et al. 2010). To take just one elaboration among many, Bertlucchi and Aglioti (2010) have deployed a distinction between 'the body in the insula' and 'the body in the parietal cortex'. They end their article with a section labelled, 'How many bodies in the brain?', wherein the 'persistent use of vague concepts' is denounced in terms that echo Pailliard's and Critchley's, and the firm assertion made that 'understanding the brain processes of corporeal awareness will require' knowledge of 'the contributions of each of the 'bodies in the brain as well as their interactions' (33).

All of that having been said, the basic twofold distinction between 'body image' and 'body schema' has retained much of its explanatory power (assuming its definition is nailed down in each specific context) and remains in constant use. However, one ongoing source of possible confusion should be highlighted: the concept of 'body image' has long been in use in psychology and psychiatry.[23] Thus, it can designate how people view their bodies in terms of their respective shapes, heights and weights – attitudes influenced by a range of factors, including family attitudes, ideological traditions, and prevalent social ideals relating to appearance and behaviour. (Hence the notion of 'self-image', as current in popular culture.) In the interests of clarity, let me say that, in this Element, I shall follow the neurological usage of 'body schema', as designating – and here I seek a common denominator between varying emphases – the organized model of the self which is mapped on the brain, a neuromatrix representation which functions through a network of neurons that subserves body sensation.

During the later twentieth century, the neurologists moved the concept from the mind to the brain, a power-move and boundary demarcation of extraordinary significance. That period saw a critical widening of an already-existing division between neurology and psychiatry, which took the disciplines even farther away

---

[23] The Austrian-American researcher Paul Ferdinand Schilder (1886–1940) has been credited with establishing the term, within psychiatry, in 1923. Head was one of the influences on Schilder's *Körperschema*, as was Freud – inevitably, given his view that the ego is primarily a body ego. In the English translation and expansion of *Das Körperschema* (Schilder 1923, rpt. 2013) *schema* became *image*: Schilder 1935, rpt. 1999, *The Image and Appearance of the Human Body*. This certainly contributed to the abovementioned terminological muddle. Ramachandran and Blakeslee 1998 do not help the situation, when they credit Head and Brain with 'coining' the phrase 'body image' to describe 'the internal image and memory of one's body in space and time' (44), a definition which instead fits Head and Hughes's view of the 'body schema'.

from each other and from nineteenth-century norms:[24] Alois Alzheimer (1864–1915) was a psychiatrist and neuropathologist, and those two major pioneers of clinical neuroscience, Pierre Broca (1824–80) and Carl Wernicke (1848–1905), had 'moved freely between the subject areas that are now delimited by neurology, neuropathology, psychiatry and psychology: their intimate interconnection was taken for granted' (Zeman 2014, 136). Things were very different in the 1990s – 'The Decade of the Brain', a golden age for neurology. Several researchers rode the crest of that wave, particularly Ramachandran and Melzack, both of whom demonstrated a talent for popularizing difficult science. Ramachandran explains the key concept of what I am calling 'body schema' as follows: 'each of us has an internally hard-wired image of the body and limbs at birth – an image that can survive indefinitely, even in the face of contradictory information from the senses' (Ramachandran & Blakeslee 1998, 42). Including information that a limb has been lost: despite this physical fact, the brain may keep on insisting that it still exists, by experiencing sensations which apparently emanate from it. Nowadays, such sensations are recognized as not being limited to limbs. They have been 'reliably described following surgery to remove the nose, tongue, teeth, anus, penis, nipples, and breast. Internal organs are not exempt; some patients even report the sensation of a full bladder and the feeling of urinating despite removal of the bladder' (Halligan 2002, 253; Arcadi 1977). Sometimes pain is associated with such sensations, of course, but not invariably – feelings of awareness may be experienced which are not necessarily unpleasant, and indeed considerable pleasure may be enjoyed, as in the curious cases of men and women with phantom feet who, when having sex, enjoy enhanced orgasms in which their phantoms participate (Ramachandran & Blakeslee, 1998, 35–8). Here the whole issue of how phantom sensations should be categorized and labelled is being presented in a particularly striking form.

Which raises the difficult question, how exactly is pain being defined here, and who makes the definitions? Crawford has gone so far as to claim that 'the exceptionally vital ghost member was remarkably pleasant until around 1980' (Crawford 2014, 76). That being the time at which, to judge by the reporting, 'phantom pain became widespread' – not coincidental, in her view, with the growth of an 'intensifying culture of pain and the rise of pain medicine in the United States broadly speaking' (82). 'Pain became an object of scientific and

---

[24] Thereby 'massive institutional barriers' were erected between 'mindless neurology' and 'brainless psychiatry', a state of affairs lamented by several contemporary researchers, who have proclaimed the inseparability of neurological and psychiatric disorders, and called for greater collaboration between the two professions. Zeman 2014, 137–8, 143; see also White, Rickards & Zeman 2012. The suspicion which both professions harbour for philosophy does not seem like evaporating any time soon.

biomedical inquiry of distinct importance' (77; she has The McGill Pain Questionnaire in mind) as well as becoming a big business – the pharmaceutical industry burgeoned, creating a vast array of medications. There is no pain without gain, certainly for Big Pharma.

But how could pain possibly not be a feature of the loss of body parts, which often occurs in the most violent and traumatizing of circumstances? To think otherwise seems counter-intuitive. Unsurprisingly, the personified phantom limb in Christine Brooke-Rose's short story 'The Foot' sadistically torments its female owner with 'unendurable' pain: 'She cries much more than quietly now, she shouts, she sobs, she yells, she gasps. I find it very exciting' (Brooke-Rose 1970, 49–50).[25] Yet, we have the facts of those pleasurable feelings noted above, and in a 1956 article Marianne Simmel reports one of her patients as saying, of his phantom limb, 'the leg felt good . . . real good' (Simmel 1956, 76). (For comparable examples, see Bourke 2014a, 70, and, for an examination of non-painful PL sensations in relation to neural changes, see Andoh et al. 2017.) This prompts the thought that, rather than 'pain being in the brain', it has been in the brains of certain neurologists, clinicians and consumers of pharmaceuticals. Phantom pain, as such, was sparsely recorded until the 1980s. An inconvenient truth, for which an explanation has been sought in the hypothesis that, before then, patients were under-reporting their mysterious condition, for fear of 'being thought foolish or insane by family, friends, practitioners, or others' (Crawford 2014, 79). Indeed, there is abundant evidence that worry about being pronounced mentally ill, and thereby disgracing one's family, inhibited many a sufferer. And if patients were reticent about reporting phantom pain, how much more so might they have been about reporting phantom pleasure?

Recent neurological research has made it quite clear that patients experiencing phantom pleasure are neither foolish nor insane. To some extent, our 'body schema' may be modified by experience, as when the brain 're-maps' certain neurological functions, this being an aspect of what is now known within neuroscience as functional integration (in opposition to the older functional specificity/segregation theory, the location of a given function in one brain region).[26] For instance, when the area in the brain mapped to an arm

---

[25] In a brilliant *coup de théâtre*, Brooke-Rose reveals the narrator as the amputee herself, who has given the phantom limb voice in order to exorcise it. Just as one seeks to separate from an abusive lover (here a veritable demon lover). The phantom is imagined as a male 'possessing' the body of a beautiful young woman. Brooke-Rose was well informed about PLS, thanks to a contact at Queen Mary's Hospital, Roehampton.

[26] 'Although it has long been assumed that cognitive functions are attributable to the isolated operations of single brain areas', Bressler and Menon (2010) write, 'the weight of evidence has now shifted in support of the view that cognition results from the dynamic interactions of distributed brain areas operating in large-scale networks'.

is, following its amputation, deprived of the sensory inputs it was used to receiving, the face area of the brain map – which happens to occupy the space on the map immediately adjacent to the space corresponding to the hand area – takes over the work once performed by the hand area, producing sensations which seem to originate in the now-missing member (Ramachandran & Blakeslee 1998, 33). A similar explanation may be offered for the results of a recent study in which one-third of 'women with radical mastectomies tested reported tingling, erotic sensations in their phantom nipples when their earlobes were stimulated' (37). Neurons relating to the nipple and the ear are located next to each other in the cerebral cortex. So, then, here is another case of re-mapping, with neurons being triggered to take on the functions once performed by their neighbours on the 'Penfield Map' in relation to the now-missing member. Furthermore, Ramachandran speculates, here is an explanation of why for many women the earlobe is an erogenous zone (Ramachandran & Blakeslee 1998, 37; see further Algioti et al. 1994). In the case of those enhanced orgasms, once again this can be explained by neuronal network reorganization; in the cerebral cortex, the neurons relating to the feet are close to those relating to the genitals.

Heady stuff. But now this seems to be an oversimplification of the brain's secrets. It has convincingly been argued that 'the perceptual changes' involved in such processes 'go beyond what can be explained by shifts in neighbouring cortical representational zones' (Knecht et al. 1996, 1213; compare the results of Grüsser et al. 2004). Further, the 'trigger zones' in question do 'not appear to be stable and can change drastically over months', and indeed can 'be located in body parts represented in clearly nonadjacent cortical areas' (Brugger 2006, 174; see further Flor 2002). So, then, the initial 'great excitement about the apparent somatotopy of referred sensations' (as Brugger puts it) has been muted by such subsequent research. But even more exciting is the ongoing revelation that the brain's system of triggering and cross-referencing, its ability to take over and execute functions once performed by some other part of its neural network, is more complicated than was imagined by some in the 1990s.

In sum, there definitely is a measure of plasticity in the brain's 'body schema', however much its extent and workings may be disputed. (More on that later.) Yet it has the qualities of stability and permanence. Witness the fact (as noted previously) that people congenitally lacking limbs can experience well-formed mental images which encompass complete bodies. It would seem that, in some measure, the 'body schema' is genetically determined, though other factors are believed to be in play, as when an amputee's 'mirror neurons' (which map the actions and intentions of others into one's own brain) enable them to experience sensations which are prompted by the sight of another person's intact body.[27] 'Mirror neuron activity may thus both require and reinforce the representation of the body and its functions within the body schema' (Cipriani et al. 2011).

The crucial point is that we can be confident of the schema's endurance until the end of our lives, and its robust transmission to our children, irrespective of how many limbs they may bring with them into the world. Here is a feature of the brain which seems to prioritize corporeal completeness, and may be judged an essential aspect of the human condition. Even though this schema

> is constructed from evanescent and fragmentary evidence derived from multiple sensory systems – vision, proprioception, hearing, etc. – we have a stable internal mental construct of a unitary corporeal self that endures in space and time, at least until its eventual annihilation in death. (Ramachandran & Hirstein 1998, 1622)

But what if it is not annihilated in death?

At one point, Ramachandran declares that the experiments he undertook to 'understand what is going on in the brains of patients with phantoms' convey a 'deeper message': '*Your own body* is a phantom, one your brain has temporarily constructed . . .' (Ramachandran & Blakeslee 1998, 58). But what if that construction of the brain, far from being temporary in the sense that it is doomed to perish with the body, survives to guide the soul in its disembodied afterlife? Here we may recall the testimony of one of the most famous amputees in British history, Horatio Nelson (d. 1805). The Vice-Admiral felt the fingers of his amputated arm quite distinctly: 'which you see', said he, 'is a direct proof of the existence of the soul, and makes the thing quite clear' (Holland 1852–54, ii.27). That prompts the question, what can phantom limb sensation, as prompted by missing body parts, tell us about the sensations experienced when the entire body is missing, severed from its soul by death? Time to bring into play the expertise of one of the greatest authorities on the nature of the soul, St Augustine of Hippo (354–430), whose influence on Western thought has been immense, moulding Christian doctrine in the early Middle Ages and far beyond.

---

[27] Mirror neurons were initially identified by Rizzolatti et al. 1988 in the ventral premotor cortex in the macaque monkey. Ramachandran proceeded to investigate the role in which they may help bring phantoms limbs to life, so to speak; he has reported that amputees experience sensations in their phantom arms when merely watching another person's intact arm being touched (Ramachandran & Rogers-Ramachandran 2008). In Ramachandran 2011, he goes so far as to claim that the ability of mirror neurons to create empathy may be the very basis of civilization. A large claim indeed – and cautionary voices have been raised. See, for example, Jarrett 2012, Jarrett 2013 and Kilner & Lemon 2013.

6 Augustine's 'Body in the Soul' and the Continuity of Pain

Augustine does not discuss phantom limb sensation in particular. He had a larger issue in mind: what sensation and cognition is possible following corporeal absence far greater than that manifested by Dedlow's fragmented torso? Total amputation, so to speak. When *all* one's limbs are lost, indeed the entire body, through death, and the separated soul proceeds to an afterlife where it experiences pain or pleasure, until the time of the Final Judgment and the resurrection of the body. The saint had a term for 'body schema', *similitudo corporis*; inevitably, given the psychosomatic language then prevailing, he locates this likeness in the soul. Here, then, is a veritable 'body in the soul', a venerable ancestor of the neuroscientists' 'body in the brain'.

The historical process of transition is clear, if convoluted, a direct consequence of the hegemony the brain has attained 'as an organ of the self in the sciences of the mind and the body' (Ortega & Vidal 2007, 256).[28] 'It has symbolically incorporated the qualities of the soul, the immaterial substance par excellence', a status reflected in contemporary science fictions which depict 'successive transplantations of your brain into a younger body'. This 'imagined brain never ages' (258). Just as, in Christian tradition, the soul never ages – thus making it the obvious repository of human intelligence in life and beyond death. In neuroscience, 'the brain's body representation' can only attain the status of 'immutability' (Mezue & Makin 2017, 43). Rather a come-down from immortality – though the immortality bestowed upon the organ in science fiction may be deemed a symbolic encoding of that immutability.

To focus on immortality, the fullest treatment Augustine affords the *similitudo corporis* is in the twelfth book of his *De Genesi ad litteram*. Here he pursues an interest in what the brain/mind/soul/psyche experiences about the body during sleep and those out-of-body experiences which in Augustine's time were known as ecstasies and nowadays are sometimes referenced as OBEs.[29] The fundamental argument is that circumstances wherein the regular functioning relationship between body and soul is temporarily set aside, in dreams (as commonly experienced) and OBEs (as extraordinarily experienced), give us a clear indication of how our soul will continue to live, using corporeal images, when it is permanently detached from the body by death.

---

[28] Contemplating the long history of ideas wherein the soul was regarded as a second or 'subtle' body, Thomas Metzinger suggests that such an entity does indeed exist – not made of 'angel stuff' or 'astral matter' but as 'pure information, flowing in the brain', the 'embodied brain's self-model' (Metzinger 2009, 257).

[29] Metzinger speculates that it was 'the particular phenomenal content of OBEs' that led human beings to belief in the existence of the soul. 'Given the epistemic resources of early mankind', he writes, it 'was a highly rational belief to assume the possibility of disembodied existence'. This step was made possible by the human brain's 'phenomenal self-model'. Metzinger 2005, 80–1.

Sometimes we regret waking up from pleasant dreams in which we were 'set among things we had always longed to have', Augustine says, while at other times we awaken 'terrified out of our wits and subjected to frightful tortures', afraid to 'go to sleep again in case we should be fetched back into the same horrors' (*DGAL* xii, 32,61; tr. Hill 2002, 501–2). Even more telling, he claims, is the testimony of those who have had OBEs,[30] the prime example of which, in the Christian tradition, was St Paul's being 'caught up to the third heaven' (II Corinthians 12:2–3). Here Augustine is referring to experiences which in contemporary neuropsychiatry are termed 'autoscopic'. Subjects 'see themselves' – though more than the visual sense is involved – as being separated from their physical bodies, experiencing an 'illusory separation between self and body' (Brugger & Mohr 2009, 137).[31] Augustine testifies that people 'who have been detached from the senses of the body, less totally indeed than if they had actually died, but still more profoundly than if they were just asleep', have 'described much more vivid sights and experiences than if they had been describing dreams'. Being 'carried away from the body's senses' and 'lain there as if they were dead', they have witnessed the pains of hell. The sights experienced in these cases are 'not bodily sights but sights resembling bodily ones' – and yet real joy and real affliction are involved (*DGAL* xii, 32,61; tr. Hill 2002, 500).

How is this possible? Because, Augustine suggests, the souls in question

> have borne in themselves some likeness to their own bodies (*similitudinem corporis sui*), by means of which it was possible for them to be carried away to those places and to experience such things with something like their senses. And I cannot see in any case why the soul should not have a likeness of its body when, with its body lying there senseless but still not totally dead [i.e. in an OBE], it sees such things as many people have told of on being restored to the living . . ., and not to have it when death overtakes it and it quits the body for good. (*DGAL* xii, 32,60; tr. Hill 2002, 499–500)

Not, then, with the bodily senses – but with *something like* them. And those souls have not experienced actual 'bodily sights but sights *resembling* bodily ones'. This raises the crucial question: what insights can we draw from this evidence about life after death? If the soul can see such things when its body is lying 'senseless but still not totally dead', why cannot it also have such vision 'when death overtakes it and it quits the body for good'? The soul may

---

[30] Cf. his earlier discussion at *De Genesi ad litteram*, xii, 5,13; Hill 2002, 469–70.
[31] See further Blanke & Mohr 2005; Brugger, Regard & Landis 1997; and Dening & Berrois 1994.

well maintain, continue to possess, the previously mentioned *similitudo corporis*, 'which is not bodily but like a body, even in the nether world'.[32]

Thus Augustine deftly shifts from the worlds of dreams and autoscopic phenomena to the nether world. Knowing how in dreams we perceive ourselves to be sitting, walking and so forth, even though our bodies are not actually engaged in those actions, helps us understand how, after death, we shall perceive bodily pain or pleasure and suffer or rejoice accordingly – not corporeally but spiritually (*DGAL* xii, 32,61; tr. Hill 2002, 501). For this process, the 'body schema' is crucial. Several recent studies have recorded a high number of amputees who recalled having an intact body representation in their dreams (Bekrater-Bodmann et al. 2015; Bekrater-Bodmann 2016; Brugger 2008; Mulder et al. 2008). This affords support to neurological speculation concerning the existence of a whole 'body in the brain', which would explain why 'the absence of inputs' from missing limbs 'does not stop the networks from generating messages' that affirm corporeal completeness and integrity (Halligan 2002, 262). It is not much of a conceptual stretch from the phantom sensation of a missing limb to the phantom sensation of a missing body.[33] Indeed, the latter may be likened to a 'globalized phantom-limb experience' (Metzinger 2005, 59).

According to Peter Brugger, who has investigated the phantoms of congenitally missing body parts, phantom limb and phantom body form a conceptual

---

[32] When Augustine returns to the subject of mental imagery in *De civitate Dei* (xviii,18), he writes, 'I believe that in thoughts or dreams there is a phantom of a man (*phantasticum hominis*) which assumes various forms through the influence of circumstances of innumerable kinds. This is not itself a body, yet, with wondrous speed, it takes on shapes which are like material bodies' (tr. Dyson 1998, 843; with alterations). Elsewhere Augustine recounts the dream-vision of a reputable physician called Gennadius, wherein a young man appears to him, to demonstrate the existence of the soul's afterlife by comparison with dream-experience. 'While you are asleep and lying on your bed these eyes of your body are now unemployed and doing nothing', says the apparition, 'and yet you have eyes with which you behold me, and enjoy this vision'. Just so, 'after your death, while your bodily eyes shall be wholly inactive, there shall be in you a life by which you shall still live, and a faculty of perception by which you shall still perceive'. Augustine refers his correspondent to the twelfth book of *De Genesi ad litteram* – presumably to its account of the *similitudo corporis* (Letter 159 to Evodius, ch. 4; *PL*, XXXIII, cols 698–701). Here is a remarkable instance of a phantom giving a tutorial on the workings of phantomology.

[33] But, as Wade 2009 says, even though the step 'from beyond the body to being completely out of it', from phantom limb to phantom body, might seem 'a short one', in fact 'the histories of their interpretations have differed radically. ... Both sets of phenomena can be interpreted in supernatural terms, but phantom limbs have proved more amenable to incorporation within the body of normal science' (243). Research into OBEs, heautoscopy and autoscopic hallucinations has had to contend with the demeaning association of such phenomena with spiritualism and psychical chicanery of the kind which Weir Mitchell despised. Metzinger has sought to afford accounts of autoscopic experience a respected place within neuropsychiatric research, arguing for a 'neurophenomenological reduction of paranormal belief systems' (Metzinger 2009, 257) which releases the subject from its dubious history and places it on a sound and respected scientific footing.

unity, both falling within the category of what he memorably calls 'phantomology': 'the science of the body-in-the-brain, a body which manifests itself, on the phenomenological level, as phantom phenomena' (Brugger 2015). Here Brugger repurposes a term used by Stanislaw Lem in his *Summa Technologiae* (1964). What we are dealing with is not (as in Lem's formulation) 'artificial reality', i.e. what nowadays is usually called 'virtual reality' in the sense of an alternative to the real thing, but rather the thing itself, reality as created and controlled by the brain. Augustine would, no doubt, have been thrilled to hear such a theory, and one might imagine him remarking that, in the restoration miracles illustrated previously, divine agency takes the soul's messaging of an intact body and turns it into reality – and then proceeding to claim that the soul's cognitive processes also draw on that innate body model beyond the grave.[34] The *similitudo corporis* is the body's representative in the soul, a body which manifests itself as phantom phenomena. Those phantom phenomena are a continuous feature of the life of the soul, manifesting themselves in dreams and OBEs in this life and continuing to operate posthumously; since the soul is eternal, they too are eternal.

To return to Augustine's own discourse, the *similitudo corporis*, his iteration of the 'body in the soul', makes use of the *imaginatio* (the faculty which creates *imagines*, *phantasmata*) to create immaterial images of material things in dreams. It functions even more vigorously in ecstasies and can be expected to be yet more vigorous when the separated soul continues its existence in the absence of the body. Thanks to its 'body schema', 'the self can be detached from the body and can live a phantom existence on its own, as in an out-of-body experience' (Brugger, qtd. by Blakeslee 2006). According to Augustine, the self can live a phantom existence following its detachment from the body in death. Here he finds an answer to the issue of the continuity of sensation from this world to the next. Because of its inbuilt *similitudo corporis*, the constant presence of a 'body in the soul', the soul takes its pains and pleasures with it – and its capacity to suffer or to celebrate will find a multitude of stimuli in hell or heaven (depending on its divinely-assigned destination). This theory affords a cogent solution to the problem faced by Augustine: not how to relieve pain but rather how to rationalize its continuation.

---

[34] Frank & Lorenzoni 1989 have posited that 'phantom limb sensations in the waking state are almost always represented only tactually, whereas this sensation in dreams is mostly represented optically as well as tactually' (186–7). Vision is very much to the fore in Augustine's account, but it should be noted that he does not regard the images in question as exclusively visual. Rather Augustine is using the term *imago* as 'shorthand for immaterial sensory impressions involving all the senses'. *All* 'the sensory attributes of a material thing encountered in regular life, touch, taste, smell, and appearance, can … be referred to as an image, or more precisely as part of the image'. Barbezat 2013, 19.

7 Augustine's 'Body in the Soul' Defended and Derided

The passage from *De Genesi ad litteram* wherein Augustine talks about the *similitudo corporis* was incorporated into the *Libri sententiarum* which Peter Lombard initially compiled c. 1154–58 (*IV Sent.*, dist. 44, 7 (257), 3; tr. Silano 2007–10, iv. 243).[35] During the 1220s at the University of Paris, this came to be established as *the* major theological textbook, and Paris, the capital city of medieval theology, set the trend for other places of learning throughout Western Europe. Every budding theologian had to comment on Augustine's doctrine of how the soul thinks and feels; it simply could not be avoided. Moreover, it enjoyed a full re-articulation in another treatise of the twelfth century, *De spiritu et anima*, a popular pseudo-Augustinian text which is probably of Cistercian origin and which certainly expresses Cistercian spirituality.[36] Here we are assured that the soul withdraws from the body 'taking with it all its faculties: sense knowledge, imagination, reason, understanding and intelligence, the concupiscible and irascible powers. And from these, the soul passes over to either joy or pain' (*DSEA* 15; Migne *PL* 40, 791). This is supported by a powerful elaboration of the Augustinian *similitudo corporis*, expressed in more straightforward language than the saint himself had used:

> Now, the soul is not a body, since not everything that is like a body is actually a body. When you sleep something like a body may appear which is not your body, but your soul. Nor is it a true body, rather the likeness of your body (*similitudo corporis*). While your body is reclining that likeness can be walking about. Your bodily tongue may be silent, the likeness will speak. Even if your eyes are shut, the likeness has vision. And so in that likeness you can recognize a detailed replica of your flesh. In that likeness your soul can wander over familiar or unknown places, capable of feeling joy or sadness. In the likeness of its body the soul of a dead man, like that of a sleeping man, can experience good and bad things. The things to which souls deprived of bodies become attached, for better or for worse, are not corporeal, but similar to corporeal things. (*DSEA* 23; Migne *PL* 40, 796–7; tr. McGinn 1977, 215, used with alterations)

Many of the thirteenth century's greatest schoolmen reacted vehemently against those ideas. In his commentary on the Lombard's *Libri sententiarum*, Albert the Great (d. 1280) writes contemptuously of those who wish to propound the belief that the separated soul 'sees and hears and imagines, and bears with it the corporeal imaginations which it received whilst in the body'; he can't be bothered to talk about how they prove this, for it is a silly proposition (Minnis

---

[35] I have used the Latin text by the Grottaferrata editors (1971–81).

[36] Its attribution to Alcher of Clairvaux is now widely discounted, though Cistercian origin remains a strong possibility. See McGinn (1977), 63–74.

2020, 149–50). In his own *Sentences* commentary, Aquinas declares that *De spiritu et anima* 'is ascribed to a Cistercian who compiled it from Augustine's works and added things of his own' (125 n. 18),[37] thereby undermining its authority. Elsewhere he engages in blatant denigration of the treatise by saying, 'what is written in it can be disregarded as lightly as it was expressed to begin with' (*Summa theologiae*, 1a, qu. 77, art. 8, ad 1).[38] But *De spiritu et anima* could not be disregarded lightly and was not going to go away. After all, many of its claims were supported by what the authentic Augustine had said, particularly in *De Genesi ad litteram*. But it was often claimed that there Augustine had merely been speculating, quoting ideas but not asserting them as his own. There is some truth in that, given Augustine's tentative rather than affirmative, explorative rather than declarative, method of procedure in the relevant discussion. However, it became a convenient means of evading direct confrontation with unwelcome views. Thus the saint was treated deferentially even as the impact of his concept of the *similitudo corporis* was lessened.

Witness, for example, the way Aquinas treats the connection Augustine had made between the way we see bodies when asleep or during more traumatic experiences, and the way the separated soul may see images of bodies (Minnis 2020, 69–70). Aquinas claims that frequently in *De Genesi ad litteram* Augustine speaks 'as one inquiring and not deciding', thereby excusing him from the rash claim (as Aquinas understands it) that a viable comparison may be made between the soul of a sleeper and the separated soul. This cannot be done, Aquinas asserts, because the sleeper's soul uses the corporeal organ of imagination whereby corporeal similitudes are imprinted, following sensory perception of the outside world. But this cannot be said of the separated soul, since it lacks that corporeal organ and is deprived of contact with that world.

The Augustinian and pseudo-Augustinian teaching at issue here stood in direct and robust opposition to the Aristotelian noetics of which Albert and Aquinas were stout defenders. The virulence of their remarks about *De spiritu et anima* obliquely testifies to the continuing strength of a spiritual tradition which was in crucial ways contrary to theirs and posed a major challenge it.[39] In fact, when handling the subversive thought of the thinker they honoured with the epithet '*the* Philosopher', they had their work cut out, given Aristotle's inconvenient belief that when a human body ceases to perform its normal life

---

[37] Alexander of Hales (d. 1245) and Bonaventure (d. 1274) accepted the attribution to Augustine (the text's Neoplatonism made it attractive to Franciscans) and drew on the treatise substantially.

[38] I have used the Blackfriars edition; Aquinas, *Summa theologiae* (1964–81).

[39] Thus Constant Mews has judiciously characterized *De spiritu et anima* as 'offering a vision of the human person influenced by Platonist tradition, before the writings of Aristotle on the soul and its powers had become widely known'. Even after Aristotle's writings had become widely known, it held its ground. Mews 2018, 343.

functions, its functional form (the soul) no longer exists. The soul dies with the body; there is no 'body in the soul', no sensation or perception beyond the grave.[40]

Much intellectual energy was expended on getting around that. Since Aristotle did not believe in a future General Resurrection, the question of posthumous experience was a simple one for him: at death the body together with all its sensory faculties perished completely, never to return. His scholastic successors were tasked with explaining not only what the separated soul could do before it rejoined its body but also how those operations related to what it would do following that reunion, when the senses would be reactivated. The notion that the resurrected body's powers had to start up from scratch was difficult if not impossible to rationalize in philosophical terms and justify in theological terms. (Will God have to engage in a second creation of humankind, make many Adams and Eves afresh?) And so, the schoolmen hit on the awkward though plausible-enough idea that, within the separated soul, the principle or root (*principio vel radix*) of the sensitive powers survived, to blossom afresh when the soul rejoined its body, indeed to function more strongly and perfectly than before. As Donald Mowbray (2009) says, by this means 'the soul could be said to possess some powers of the senses', while the notion that it 'possessed some sensitive powers independent of the body' was defused (109).

This brings us to Dante, the second major protagonist of the present Element, and to one of his most daring intellectual enterprises. In *Purgatorio* XXV the shade of Statius, having been called upon to speak by Dante's spirit-guide, Virgil, attempts to explain its operations in the other world. When 'the soul is loosed from the flesh' certain faculties will become 'mute' (*mute*), but

' . . . memoria, intelligenza e volontade
in atto molto piú che prima agute'. (83–4)
['memory, intellect and will [shall be] far more acute in action than before'][41]

That is to say, the sensory and appetitive powers will be muted, since they no longer have any bodily organs with which to function. But the rational powers of memory, intelligence and will shall survive – and, indeed, be even more vigorous than before. Here Dante is designating the three rational faculties as defined in Augustinian psychology (Nardi 1960, 58).[42]

However, this has been connected to a much later doctrine, relating to the psychic state of the separated soul. In his *Summa theologiae* Aquinas claims that

---

[40] The crucial texts are *De anima*, 408b18–24 and 413a3–7; cf. Matthews (2015), 194–9. At *Nicomachean Ethics*, 1111b20–23 Aristotle says that, for a human being, immortal life is simply an impossibility, and no amount of wishing can alter that fact.

[41] All *Comedy* references are to Petrocchi (1994). I have drawn on the translation included in Singleton (1977).

[42] Cf. Augustine, *De Trinitate*, x, 11; also xii, 15, and xiv, 7–8.

when the soul leaves the body, the sensory powers do not remain in the soul actually (*actu*) but only virtually (*virtute tantum*), as in their principle or root (*in principio vel radice*; *Summa theologiae*, 1a, qu. 77, art. 8, 1 and ad. 1). In other words, they are turned off for the duration. This is not the same as saying that they have been shut down completely – far from it. Speculation here was limited by the necessity of affirming their reactivation (and, indeed, their enhanced functioning) following the return of the body, duly perfected, at the General Resurrection. But what happens in the meantime? As Aquinas answers this question in his *Summa contra Gentiles* (II, 80–1, 12), the 'soul's operations which are not exercised through bodily organs certainly remain in the soul when it leaves the body'. Indeed, 'the more the soul is freed from preoccupation with its body, the more fit does it become for understanding higher things' (Minnis 2020, 123). The body in question being, of course, the human body as at present constituted.

On the face of it, this seems to fit well with what Dante is saying. But – and this is the crucially important point – Aquinas makes his claim in the context of asserting that 'the soul understands in a different manner when it is separated from the body'. 'The mode of understanding vouchsafed to us in the present life' will cease 'upon the death of the body', to be replaced by 'another and higher mode of understanding' – by which Aquinas means the reception of knowledge from above, divine infusion, as occurs in the case of angels. However, in *Purgatorio* XXV Dante is more interested in the cognitive processes of human souls than those of angels.

8 Reluctant Prostheses: The Aerial Embodiments of Angels

Angels have been appearing to humans throughout history, according to Jewish, Christian and Muslim traditions of long standing. Within Christianity, undoubted the most important appearance is that of the angel Gabriel before the Virgin Mary, to announce that she will be the mother of Christ (Luke 1:26–38). In an extraordinarily popular late-medieval devotional text, the *Meditationes vitae Christi* (c. 1300),[43] we read that, 'rejoicing and exulting, Gabriel flew down from high, and was in an instant in human form (*in humana specie*) and face to face with the Virgin, who was then in the bedroom of her little house' (Stallings-Taney 1997, 20). Mary was well used to visits from angels, we are assured, but this was a very special occasion. The frequency of Mary's communications with those spiritual creatures is understandable, given her destiny as 'the Mother of God'. However, everyone was supposed to have

---

[43] The date and authorship of this treatise remain matters of dispute. For a recent discussion, see Tóth & Falvay 2014.

a guardian angel, a notion which goes back to Ancient Judaism and was eagerly developed within Christianity. To take one example among many, from the *Liber specialis gratiae* of the Cistercian nun Mechthild of Hackeborn (d. 1298), at the time of the Feast of St Michael the Archangel, Mechthild witnesses 'a host of angels in attendance' during mass. 'Each one stood by the virgin entrusted to him [i.e. beside his special nun] in the form of a beautiful young man' (*Liber specialis gratiae*, i.30; tr. Newman 2017, 108).

But why exactly would an angel wish to make itself known *in humana specie*, or, indeed, as a beautiful young man? An explanation of that, and many other issues appertaining to the symbolism of angelic manifestation, is provided in *The Celestial Hierarchy* of Pseudo-Dionysius the Areopagite, a Christian Neoplatonist of the late fifth or early sixth century who enjoyed great authority because he was mistakenly identified as the Athenian convert of St Paul mentioned in Acts 17:34. Here the fundamental idea is that a masculine image is an appropriate form for such a superior creature to adopt, given man's position at the very top of the hierarchy of creation postulated in Genesis; Adam is at once the ruler of the natural world and a creature with the highest spiritual aspirations, having been made in the *imago Dei*. Hence Pseudo-Dionysius affirms that man is 'intelligent and capable of looking toward the higher things. Sturdy and upright, he is, by nature, a leader and ruler.... [I]t is he who dominates all with the superior power of his intelligence' (Luibheid 1987, 184–5). But why do angels sometimes appear as youthful? This indicates 'the perennial vigor' of their 'living power' (Luibheid 1987, 184–5). Why do they have wings? Because 'wings signify their uplifting swiftness, the climb to heaven, the ever-upward journey whose constantly upward thrust rises above all earthly longing' (186). Furthermore, 'the lightness of wings symbolizes the freedom from all worldly attraction, their pure and untrammelled uplifting towards the heights'. They have the power of hearing attributed to them because this signifies their degree of awareness, 'the ability to have a knowing share of divine inspiration' (185). In all of those (and many other) examples, there is nothing functional about the attributes of angels. For instance, they do not need wings to fly; those appurtenances are there to signal some aspect of their immaterial existence. But how, then, do they manage to communicate with creatures who, in this life at least, *are* material and whose senses are unable to perceive beings that lack material form?

The answer is that they take on bodies of air. Here we encounter yet another tradition of long standing, as attested (for example) by the *Etymologiae* of Isidore of Seville (d. 636). Discussing the nature of the pagan gods (demons who are identified as fallen angels), Isidore explains that they 'flourish in accordance with the nature of aerial bodies' (VIII.xi.16–17; Barney et al. 2006, 184). Hardly a dense form of material, to be sure, but it does afford sufficient visibility, while signifying an unearthly existence. An 'angel can assume a body from any element, as well as from several elements mixed together', Aquinas assures us (Minnis 2020, 98). But air is the best one to use, since it 'condenses easily so as to take and retain shape and reflect various colours from other bodies, as may be seen in the clouds'. Air 'can be condensed in one part more, in another less, in another least of all, thereby being shaped like nerve, bone and flesh', Bonaventure explains; 'it can in one part intercept more light, in another less, in another least of all', thereby displaying diverse colours: thus in every way conforming to a human body (*In II Sent.*, dist. viii, pars 1, art. 2, qu. 2).[44]

From pliable air, then, angels fashion human shapes and facsimiles of human organs, in order to be seen by human beings and to converse with them. There are many examples in Scripture of angels speaking through their assumed bodies, Aquinas notes. But this is a matter of appearance. Angels do not speak as such; they merely 'imitate speech, forming sounds in the air corresponding to human words' (*Summa theologiae*, 1a, qu. 51, art. 3, ad 4). When speech is ascribed to them this is 'not really natural speech but an imitation thereof by producing a like effect: and the same applies to eating' (Minnis 2020, 141 n. 24). As spiritual creatures, 'pure form' (Elliott 1991, 134), angels definitely do not need to eat, not requiring any material food to sustain themselves. The 'eye' in an aerial body is not used for the purpose of seeing, says Bonaventure, but rather because the lack thereof would look strange on a face that resembles a human's, and infringe the quality of perfection which is associated with the angelic form (*In II Sent.*, dist. viii, pars 1, art. 3, qu. 2). Through an assumed body angels do not, or cannot, exercise the acts of sensing, he continues, even though that body may possess all the human organs. In sum, aerial bodies are not naturally joined to angels, as the human soul is joined to its body, giving it life and functioning through, and with, the senses. Rather, those spiritual creatures merely *assume* bodies of air, to instruct and protect us. Peter Lombard sums up the matter succinctly: 'At God's disposition, at times they take on bodies in order to perform a service commanded to them by God, and they set them aside when their service is completed. It was in such bodies that they appeared and spoke to men' (*II Sent.*, dist. 8, ch. 1 (43), 3; tr. Silano 2007–10, ii.34–5).

So, then, the job having been done, the aerial body is discarded. With a certain relief, presumably; angels do not desire that temporary body, take pleasure in it, need it for any purpose of their own. It is rather a come-down for a superior creature to take on an inferior shape, to clothe itself in matter which it must

---

[44] I have used the edition by the Quaracchi editors (1882–1902), vol. ii.

cumbrously move to enact certain functions (but *not* animate in the way in which a human soul animates its body); in the process, it compromises the freedom and mobility which, as a spiritual creature, it normally would enjoy. As far as angels are concerned, then, aerial body parts are blatantly artificial rather than natural. Although eager to serve the divine will in carrying out the tasks assigned to them, it might be said that they engage in self-prosthesis with a degree of reluctance.

9 Eager Prostheses: The Aerial Embodiments of Separated Souls

Angels do not know what it's like to be human, and don't need or want to know. They are strangers to the human mental processes and emotions. *Experientia*, rightly understood, 'belongs to the senses', Aquinas declares (*De malo*, qu. xvi, art. 1, ad 2, ed. Regan & Davies 2001, 814–15). Angels have never shared the experience of embodiment, and therefore can neither understand how human souls sense and think through bodily organs nor appreciate their overwhelming desire to be reunited with those same organs. Medieval theologians commonly argued that, no matter how happy the saints may be in heaven at the moment, their joy shall increase when they are reunited with their bodies. Little wonder, then, that in *Purgatorio* XXV Statius and his familiars (whose sources of happiness, in purgatory, fall far short of the pleasures of heaven) should be so motivated to engage in premature or anticipatory resurrections – as their mental 'body schemas' move beyond the production of mental phantoms to take on aerial phantoms of human bodies, *ombre*.

Angels, of course, lack such human 'body schemas', as spiritual beings without materiality. (And PLP must be unknown to creatures that don't just lack limbs but never have had them.) As noted previously, when angels visited humans they were supposed to have taken on bodies of air, in order to be witnessed and perceived. Dante has gone beyond theological tradition to extend this ability to separated souls.

> 'così l'aere vicin quivi si mette
> e in quella forma ch'è in lui suggella
> virtüalmente l'alma che ristette' (*Purgatorio* XXV, 94–6)
> ['so there, where the soul stopped, the nearby air takes on
>   the form that the soul virtually impressed upon it']

These imprints of soul on air enable the Dante-persona to see them. There is no indication, however, that this show is being put on for his unique benefit; it seems to be a regular feature of life in purgatory. Statius and his associates certainly have an abundance of material near at hand, that yielding, pliable 'nearby air' which subjects itself to the creation of human shapes.

Never has a more ideal prosthetic substance been available. A fact recognized, and indeed extolled, by Saint Augustine. The aerial body is the 'finest, nimblest kind of body there is', he says (*De divinatione daemonum*, iv,6; Migne *PL* 40, 586–7; tr. Hill 2005, 207). Just imagine what can be done with it! 'There are some human beings who with the coarser material at their disposal', including 'earth and water, stone and various metals, can do such amazing things that those who lack any ability are frequently dumbfounded'. When actual divine agency is involved, the achievements are even more amazing. 'Just ask yourself how much more prodigious and amazing must be the things demons [and angels, of course] can do'. Air, then, is infinitely more malleable than any of the Civil War contraptions of wood, metal and leather, or indeed the contemporary technological marvels which deploy acrylics, epoxies, fiberglass and Kevlar, and extend to microprocessor knees with hydraulic systems.[45] It is tempting to compare the liquid but quickly solidifying metal that forms the shape-shifting body of the advanced Terminator T-1000 in the award-winning movie *Terminator 2: Judgment Day* (1991).[46] By shaping its fluid material accordingly this humanoid can create all the human limbs and sensory facilities,[47] being able to hear and speak (in various assumed voices). All of those powers are enhanced, stronger versions of human capabilities. But Dante (backed up by much medieval theology) got there first. However, as a building material air is diaphanous, mist-like and appropriate to its spiritual surroundings, quite unlike the hard, unyielding surfaces with which the T-1000 conducts its lethal business.

There is evidence aplenty of the phantom limbs of amputees welcoming their material replacements (Herrmann & Gibbs 1945; Hoffman 1954; Sobchack 2006; see also Crawford 2014, 11; for complications, see Funk & Brugger 2008). That is certainly the case with the phantoms of *Purgatorio* XXV, who experience great pleasure as they make aerial artifacts of themselves for themselves – in contrast with regular human prosthesis, where amputees must rely on the brainpower of the latest experts, the inventions of others being gifted to them. Or imposed upon them. The separated souls of *Purgatorio* XXV are their own skilled technicians, engaged in a process of self-reconstruction to create diaphanous facsimiles of complete bodies. However, any such constructions, whether the work of human souls or angels, are poor things in comparison with

---

[45] On the cultural implications of this history, see the chapter 'Phantom-Prosthetic Relations: The Modernization of Amputation' in Crawford (2014), 193–222, which addresses the issue of 'techno-induced liberation'.

[46] An American science-fiction action film produced and directed by James Cameron, starring Arnold Schwarzenegger and Linda Hamilton, and with Robert Patrick as the T-1000.

[47] Thus it can create 'the organs of every sense', even including sight: compare the artful aerial prosthesis described by Dante, discussed later in this section.

the future craftsmanship of the supreme artificer, God, who at the General Resurrection shall work with flesh, blood and bone, to at once reconstitute and improve upon the human bodies which were occupied during life. The result will be a brilliantly bright, crystalline, supremely beautiful body (not unlike the T-1000 android?). A paradoxical body indeed, which will retain all the distinguishing features it possessed during its original life, but its blood will glow as polished red gold, its animal spirits as clear light, its nerves as polished silver, while brilliant shades of gold and silver will shine through a delicate but indestructible membrane of what was once lacklustre skin (Albert the Great; qtd. by Minnis 2016, 222). This greatly enhanced human form will outshine the gleaming metal carapace of the most technically advanced robot,[48] even as it will share with that artificial intelligence the freedom from the necessities of eating, drinking and populating the planet through sexual reproduction.

Until that time of unalloyed joy, the phantoms have their pleasures. If it may be wondered how such enjoyment could possibly be admitted in a place of excruciating pain, one should recall the fact that Dante's purgatory is essentially a place of hope, its denizens being confident of future bliss. That pain is desired, embraced, taken possession of, as part of the purgative process that will render them fit for heaven.

'Dante the traveler may sometimes forget that those he encounters are mere shadows', remarks Caroline Walker Bynum, 'but Dante the poet never lets the reader forget that these are *not* the bodies of earthly or of eternal life' (Bynum 2017, 300). She adds that 'it is natural for soul to express itself in body, but ... shades are not enough' (302). This is absolutely true, in the case of the *ombre* of *Purgatorio* XXV and, indeed, of the *Comedy* as a whole. That canto contains one of the poem's great definitional moments, its psychosomatic explanation having relevance for all the self-manifestations of spirits encountered in Dante's spirit world. Yet here the *ombre* seem to be enjoying a lot of that sensory *experientia* which is unique to human beings and makes them human. On the one hand, we are dealing with artificial bodies (the point emphasized by Bynum), and hence I am deploying the term 'prosthesis' in its technical medical sense here. On the other, those aerial bodies are direct anticipations of the natural (though perfected) bodies that the souls of Statius and his companions will inhabit in the 'new heaven, new earth' (as predicted at Apocalypse 21:1). Regarded in that latter sense, we are dealing with re-embodiments on a scale far in excess of, and more profound than, those bestowed upon Peter of Grenoble, Gundrada of Soissons and John of Damascus (as described previously), all of which are pronounced to be

---

[48] Great emphasis is placed on the *claritas*, the intense brightness, of the resurrected body; this is its leading quality.

pledges and proofs of the future Resurrection. Here, then, is a prosthetic process that goes far beyond the imposition of something artificial.

The level of bodily detail achieved by Statius and his fellow-craftsmen is astonishing. Virtual organs for *all* the senses are formed out of air – even including sight. Widely regarded in Western culture as the noblest, strongest and most subtle of all the senses,[49] its presence indicates the fullness and completeness of this aerial embodiment:

> "e quindi organa poi
> ciascun sentire infino a la veduta." (101–2)
> ["therefrom it forms the organs of every sense, even to the sight."]

The *ombre* are allowed a strikingly wide range of powers. So eager are those souls for materiality that they can produce virtual bodies capable of performing actions like speaking, laughing, weeping and so forth. Medieval theologians, as we have seen, emphasized that angels are not naturally connected to the aerial bodies which they temporarily deploy. When they appear *in humana specie*, they merely move around matter which is cumbersome to them (so the usual doctrine runs), mimicking human actions such as seeing, hearing and speaking for as long as their divine mission requires (and in order to present a non-frightening image to their audiences, thereby respecting human frailty). Angels do not 'have sensations through the organs of the bodies they assume'; they cannot 'live' through them in a relationship comparable to the one whereby a human soul animates its body (Aquinas, *Summa theologiae*, 1a, qu. 51, art. 3). *Assuming* a body is a very different thing from *animating* it. Dante, however, seems to be going some distance toward suggesting that his phantoms are indeed able to animate the materials they have shaped to suit their needs.

Does he actually go that far? This is unclear. And here we must acknowledge, and give due prominence to, the common scholastic belief (well supported by the science of the day) that aerial bodies are incapable of animation. No aerial material substance can be animated, declares Aquinas; it cannot become a living thing (*De malo*, qu. xvi, art. 1, resp.; ed. Regan & Davies 2001, 814–15). Here he is talking about the inability of a demon to animate an aerial body. But *mutatis mutandis* this principle could also be applied to what a separated soul can and cannot do with its body of air. On this reckoning, then, while 'the organs of every sense' may well be formed from air, they would be incapable of functioning as actual sense organs.

But that fails to satisfy, as a reading of the relevant lines in *Purgatorio* XXV. Given the enthusiasm with which Statius proclaims the formation of sense-

---

[49] Minnis 2016, 37, 198–9, 201–2, 314 n. 261; Woolgar 2006, 23, 147–89.

organs, it seems difficult to accept that he has just in mind that mimicry of human actions which is all that angels can do (though they can put on a good show). Separated souls are not angels; they have psychosomatic needs all of their own, an extraordinarily powerful desire for embodiment which will be satisfied only at the General Resurrection. In the meantime, the creative virtue (*virtù formativa*) which they channel will exert its power to shape the neighbouring air into appealing forms (cf. lines 88–90). Arguing against the suggestion that aerial bodies can be organic, Aquinas states that 'bodies can only be organic if they in themselves can have limit and shape', a property which air lacks, given that, itself incapable of being limited, it cannot 'be distinguished from the surrounding air' (*De malo*, qu. xvi, art. 1, resp.; ed. Regan & Davies 2001, 814–15). It might be countered that the *virtù formativa* at work in *Paradiso* XXV is perfectly capable of distinguishing some part of the air from its surroundings, imposing the limits necessary for some measure of organicism.

Dante's intention on that front remains opaque. What *is* evident is that he is offering a high estimation, indeed engaging in an extraordinary celebration, of the activities which separated souls can perform. That is clearly true, I believe, irrespective of the extent to which he supposes those activities can be conducted through aerial bodies – indeed, that issue might be termed incidental, in comparison with what he is saying about what powers the soul carries with it from this life into the next. There is nothing like that in the theologies of the scholastic followers of Aristotle. However, Cistercian spirituality offers a close parallel and precedent. The latter part of *Paradiso* XXV could be seen as the apotheosis of the Augustinian *similitudo corporis*, when the 'body schema' as experienced in dreams and OBEs continues to function in the afterlife, bringing with it much of the sentient activity which it pursued during life, enabling the soul to 'wander over familiar or unknown places, capable of feeling joy or sadness' (to apply a phrase from *De spiritu et anima*, 23).

Support for this reading may be found in a gloss on *Purgatorio* XXV which Dante's learned son Pietro wrote during the period 1359–64 (ed. Chiamenti, 2002). Pietro quotes a passage from Aquinas's *Summa theologiae*, which has previously been cited in this essay, where the saint had argued that when the body-soul composite is destroyed the sensory powers remain in the soul not actually but only virtually, 'as in their principle or root (*in principio vel radice*)'. But this is juxtaposed with the opposing argument from *De spiritu et anima* (15, as quoted previously) about how the soul, on withdrawing from the body, takes all its faculties with it. Pietro immediately follows up this citation with Augustine's own advocacy of the *similitudo corporis*. Here, I suggest, we may identify the determining influence behind the latter part of *Purgatorio* XXV. And at this point it should be recalled that, in the final analysis and at the very end of his *Comedy*, Dante affords that major leader of the Cistercian order, Saint Bernard of Clairvaux, pride of place as a guide to the Empyrean Heaven, rather than Saint Albert or Saint Thomas.[50]

10 Solving the Pain Problem: It's All in the Soul

The denizens of hell could hardly share the enthusiasm of those souls temporarily in purgatory, and perpetually in heaven, for the return of their bodies. That meant another means of painful punishment being inflicted upon them, another target presented for the divine wrath. But how could separated souls, in the absence of bodies, experience pain? Was that something that had to be postponed until the General Resurrection, when the body was reconstituted? Mainstream medieval theologians could not countenance the souls of the wicked hanging around, unpunished, until then, so some other explanation had to be provided. Augustine found it in the soul's *similitudo corporis*, the mental facsimile of the material body which it contained within itself, and carried with it when it passed from this world to the next. That 'body schema' is quite capable of generating pain all on its own, without the presence of physical trauma, or of generating pleasure, again without physical stimuli. As already mentioned, *De Genesi ad litteram* (xii, 32,61) develops the theory that in dreams and OBEs we see not bodily sights but sights resembling bodies, yet nevertheless real pains and pleasures are experienced. The situation may well be similar in the other world, Augustine speculates, in places which are not bodily but like bodily places, yet where there will be real ease and rest or punishment and pain. It is the soul and not the body that is being affected, which experiences pleasure or pain. So, then, it's all in the head/psyche/soul – but nonetheless painful or pleasurable for that. The brain is capable of producing pain without any direct body stimulus, in the absence of pathological wounds – witness our Leicester builder and the psychosomatic case-histories described by O'Sullivan (2016).

But Augustine's successors robustly rejected this viewpoint. It seemed to be too much at variance with the materiality of hell-fire as asserted by other saints and the somaticizing declamations of the Old Testament prophets, as when Isaiah lxvi:24 threated sinners with unquenchable fire and Judith xvi:21 declared that God 'will give fire, and worms into their flesh, that they may burn, and may feel for ever'. A further curb was imposed on speculation by the stringent Paris University prohibitions of 1270 and 1277, which prohibited any denial that the separated soul can suffer the pains of corporeal fire (Minnis 2020, 36–7). Even though those measures are seen, quite rightly, as a move to counter

---

[50] About which, see particularly Botterill 1994.

the unbridled use of the recently-recovered Aristotelian corpus, here the Bishop of Paris who promulgated them sought to exclude a strand of thought which goes all the way back to Augustine – though the saint himself never developed the radical potential of the thought in question. It was left to *De spiritu et anima*, and certain other Cistercian treatises, to take it further.

A *via media*, of sorts, had been offered by St Gregory the Great (d. 604), who held that the soul is 'burned' inasmuch it sees itself to be burned. 'An invisible burn and an invisible pain are received from visible fire' (*Dialogi*, iv.29; Migne *PL*, 77, 368A). In other words, the fire is material but the pain is not. The very sight of that fire generates acute mental pain; the separated soul suffers from and through imaginations. Vision provokes feeling. So, then, Gregory's thinking is close to Augustine's in that sensations of extreme heat are believed to be caused by mental images of fire rather than by real fire. To see the burn, it would seem, is to feel the burn. Yet the fire itself is real, and materially comparable with the type we encounter in everyday life. And here Gregory parts company with Augustine. As Barbezat (2013, 9) puts it, 'Gregory's fire is not spiritual or imaginary, even if it is experienced that way.'

One might ask the question: What point is there in the flames being real, since the desired effect may be produced without that? To which Gregory would have to answer, they have to be real in order to trigger the required effect, even though (to put the matter in modern neurological terms) that mental reaction is totally brain-generated, rather than a reaction to bodily trauma. For there can be no bodily trauma, given that material flame cannot burn an immaterial soul; the fire has no fuel to feed on. However, Gregory's awkward attempt to 'square the circle' may be better understood if we recall the long-standing tradition that hell had a specific physical location, usually identified as 'under' (i.e. in the centre of) the earth (Minnis 2020, 54–5). This made the notion that a spiritual entity, the soul, could suffer in the presence of physical fire a lot easier to accept, because a physical location for that fire was widely assumed, and required no huge effort of justification. All of this was, of course, challenged by the Augustinian notion that, thanks to the *similitudo corporis* which it bears, the 'soul can wander over familiar or unknown places' (to echo the *De spiritu et anima* yet again), those places themselves being imaginary, though real pain or pleasure is experienced there. This happens in dreams and may be expected to happen also in the other world. However, given the demands of late-medieval scholasticism, no acceptable solution of this kind could be found. Real fire as well as real pain in a real place was demanded, material fire being a major cause of the soul's pain.

When he treats this issue, Thomas Aquinas seems totally skeptical of the idea that the mind can generate enough agony to effect the necessary punishment. He seems incapable of believing that the brain can create its own hell. For the soul to suffer not from real fire but from the mere apprehension of fire would not be sufficiently painful, in his view. Having noted that God has prepared the fires of hell for demons as well as the damned, Aquinas opines that it is highly unlikely that demons who (given their origin as angels) are endowed with subtle intelligence, would think it possible for a corporeal fire to hurt them, unless they were actually distressed by it (Minnis 2020, 68). Demons are not stupid, and do not scare easily. They are far too clever to be frightened by mere imaginations of fire. Humans are less smart, but their separated souls would similarly be unperturbed.

A solution to the problem was inevitably found, given that many of the best minds of the day were working on it. Aquinas argued that the soul is surrounded – 'enchained, in a manner of speaking' – by the fire, prevented from performing its natural functions, and thus endures acute distress (76–8). Here is a way in which a spiritual entity, the soul, can be said to experience pain caused by a material one. God's punishment is inflicted by the entrapping and confining envelope of flame, against which the soul reacts with ongoing horror, as an ignominious, debasing form of imprisonment which, for the damned, will never end. A hateful body-fire composite has been created, which stays in place, maintains its existence, in a way comparable to the soul's loving relationship with the body (though being, one might say, a gross parody of it). So, then, the sinner's soul is enveloped in fire throughout eternity, while not actually being burned. It suffers immeasurably – but from incarceration rather than incineration. Given the traditional notion that demons and the damned resided within the physical confines of hell in the earth's bowels, itself an imprisoning space, this was, perhaps, hardly a giant step to take. At any rate, it became the best solution that thirteenth-century schoolmen could offer.

It is fascinating to note that, despite the Aristotelians' massive pushback against the idea of a 'body in the soul', despite all the dismissive things they said about *De spiritu et anima*, they too came up with a theory of brain/mind/soul/psyche causing pain in the absence of somatic trauma. When arguing against the implications of the Augustinian *similitudo corporis*, Aquinas does allow that the sight of fire can cause considerable distress. But he judges this as a sort of supplement to the main event, the pain inflicted by material fire (77). Like Gregory and so many others before and after him, he supposes that the fire must be material. However, his own solution involves the soul being encased in flame which does not do it any physical harm. It's a nerve rather than a tissue problem. The soul utterly loathes being entrapped by fire, which renders its freedom of movement impossible and disgusts it inasmuch as a lowly aspect of creation has been given power over one with great eminence, nobility, and perfection.

(Rarely have feelings of entitlement and privilege been afforded so much significance.) A cause of acute pain indeed. Who needs somatic trauma, pathological wounds?

Resistance to the idea that 'The mind is its own place, and in it self / Can make a Heav'n of Hell, a Hell of Heav'n' (Milton, *Paradise Lost*, I.254–5), is directly comparable with recent refusals to accept a psychosomatic diagnosis for the many medical ailments which lack a clear explanation in physical terms. At least PLP is now being taken with the kind of seriousness it deserves. Contemporary neuroscientists have moved far away from the view of R. D. Langdale Kelham, O. B. E. (1891–1964) that it was caused by the psychological distress of someone with 'an unsatisfactory personality', an 'anxious, introspective, dissatisfied and ineffective' person who, 'becoming obsessed by his symptoms, and brooding upon them and his disability, tends to dramatise their degree, using undoubted exaggerations in his description of his sufferings' (Kelham 1952, 1231, 139; Bourke 2014a, 73–4, 78).[51]

However, in the formation of actual diagnoses, negative, uncomprehending and dismissive attitudes have persisted; no doubt our Leicester builder had some people thinking that he was unmanly, a softie, weakling, or wimp – why, the nail didn't actually hurt his foot, yet he made all that fuss! O'Sullivan's book has demonstrated that some medical practitioners, together with members of the general public and patients themselves, still 'struggle to accept the power of the mind over the body' (16). 'Many doctors think that sufferers of conversion disorders and somatic disorders have a particular sort of personality', she reports in an uncomfortable echo of Kelham's view. 'Those perceived to have the *right* sort of personality for psychosomatic disorders will be offered the diagnosis too often, and those deemed *the wrong sort* will have their diagnosis missed' (275–6). Certain biases have remained entrenched, despite the fact that – particularly in the last thirty years – the scientific and diagnostic categories and terminology have changed considerably and the intellectual context has shifted immeasurably.

11 Science and Immortality

The most obvious shift in intellectual context is the thoroughgoing secularization of society in general and of the medical profession in particular, since the time when Weir Mitchell coined the phrase 'phantom limbs'. The transition 'from prayer to painkillers' has 'dramatically changed the way people-in-pain experienced their afflictions', as Joanna Bourke has succinctly said. 'Stripped of its

---

[51] Kelham dominated the field in England during the 1950s, working in the Limb Centre at Queen Mary's Hospital, Roehampton.

mysticism and its function in nudging people towards more virtuous behavior, being-in-pain is emptied of a significant part of its positive value' (Bourke 2014b, 121, 127). This was accompanied with robust confidence in the ability of science to achieve victory over pain. The moment of change is well illustrated by a lecture on 'Science and Immortality' delivered in 1904 by William Osler (1849–1919),[52] an eminent physician whose career Weir Mitchell did much to advance.

> [W]ithin the lifetime of some of us, Science – physical, chemical, and biological – has changed the aspect of the world, changed it more effectively and more permanently than all the efforts of man in all preceding generations. (Osler 1905, 6)

What an extraordinary affirmation of the transformative power of science, its ability to create a better, more enlightened, world in the new century! Osler, who claimed the seventeenth-century polymath Sir Thomas Browne as his 'life long mentor' (4, 53), is a highly articulate witness to the intellectual cross-currents which were swirling at that time. His faith in the new science is strong, to the point of hubris – *all* the efforts of man in *all* preceding generations have been transcended! (A mere ten years later, a World War would tear civilization apart.) Yet his lecture also conveys a sense of loss. Scientists are disinterested in what may come after our lives on earth have ended. As is the general public, circa 1904. 'Over our fathers immortality brooded like the day', Osler declares, but 'we have consciously thrust it out of lives so full and busy that we have no time to make an enduring covenant with our dead' (15). For his generation, 'The dead are no longer immanent' (14).

That said, Osler admits that much of his work is 'among the brothers of Sir Galahad, and the sisters of Sir Percival, among the dreamers of dreams and the seers of visions, whose psychical vagaries often transcend the bounds of every-day experiences' (30). (Here Osler has in mind science's inquiry into the spirit-world, which, he declares, as yet has proved futile.) He proceeds to identify a small group of 'idealists', people ruled by the heart rather than the head (including Plato, Saint Bernard, Saint Francis, Saint Teresa and Cardinal Newman), who are the 'salt of the earth', rather than its 'leaven' (34–5; cf. Matthew 5:12–13). Although they may be 'prejudiced, often mistaken in worldly ways and methods, they alone have preserved in the past, and still keep for us to-day, the faith that looks through death'. Only such idealists, 'who walk by faith and not by sight', 'have ever had perfect satisfaction' on 'the question of the immortality of the soul'. But 'the new psychologists have ceased to think nobly of the soul, and even speak of it as a complete superfluity' (26).

---

[52] Sir William Osler, First Baronet, was one of the founding professors of Johns Hopkins Hospital. Originally, he had been destined for a career in the church; his father was an Anglican minister.

Weir Mitchell, whose feelings for Osler encompassed admiration and rivalry, was troubled by those sentiments. Having lived long lives wherein we improve in action and reasoning, and construct 'mental machinery of value' – surely 'it does not seem likely that all this is going to be lost?' (Mitchell qtd. by Cervetti 2012, 244). The fears of men of his education and cultural formation are well summed up in the words of a poet beloved by both medical men, Alfred Lord Tennyson (1809–92):

> My own dim life should teach me this,
> That life shall live for evermore,
> Else earth is darkness at the core,
> And dust and ashes all that is . . . .
> (*In Memoriam*, XXXIV; *Tennyson*, ed. Ricks 2007, 377)

Mitchell's recent biographer, Nancy Cervetti, characterizes him as ardently wanting 'to believe that he would continue to exist after death' (Cervetti 2012, 243, cf. 231). A desire certainly shared by his limbless creation George Dedlow, that unhappy 'fraction of a man' who is 'eager for the day' when he can 'rejoin the lost members of [his] corporeal family in another and a happier world'. At the General Resurrection, he shall become whole again, his limbs restored in reality rather than through phantom imaginings, and by divine agency rather than through illusions induced by some Sister Euphemia.

The late-medieval schoolmen on whose theology I have drawn were adamant that 'man cannot achieve his ultimate happiness unless the soul be once again united to the body' (Aquinas); 'in order for the soul's happiness to be complete, its body must return to it' (Bonaventure); 'there is not perfect blessedness before the resurrection of the body' (Giles of Rome; all qtd. in Minnis 2016, 211). But no-one has expressed the sheer joy of anticipated reunion better than Dante. In *Paradiso* XIV, speaking for all the virtuous souls in the sphere of the sun, Solomon confidently looks forward to the paradise beyond death,

> 'come la carne glorïosa e santa
> fia rivestita, la nostra persona
> più grata fia per esser tutta quanta'. (*Paradiso* XIV, 43–5)
> ['when our flesh, sanctified and glorious, shall clothe our
>   souls once more, our person then will be more pleasing
>   because it is complete']

Dante is eager to give 'the flesh which the earth still covers' (lines 55–57) its due. Its return is necessary for full personhood, and the totality of the Resurrection involves the restoration of all of a person's body parts, wherever they may be. At that time 'the dust of bodies long dead will return, with an ease and swiftness that we cannot understand, to members which are thereafter to live a life without end'. Thus Augustine (*De civitate Dei*, xx,20; tr. Dyson 1998, 1013). To borrow phrases from John Donne, 'numberless infinities / Of souls' will go to rejoin the 'scattered bodies' which have been slain by a wide range of causes (*Holy Sonnets*, VII). Including war.

Many limbs lie moldering in American Civil War graves, awaiting the glory of the coming of the Lord. Long detached from body stumps, the existence of those lost parts was vividly recalled by the phantom sensations of their haunted owners, as Mitchell's writings bring out so well. His 1871 article includes the tale of one sufferer who, on waking from sleep every morning, has 'to learn anew that my leg is enriching a Virginia wheat crop or ornamenting some horrible museum' (Mitchell 1871, 566–7).[53] A museum like the US Army Medical Museum which, according to Mitchell's fable, houses George Dedlow's legs as items 3486 and 3487. In one of Louisa May Alcott's *Hospital Sketches* (1863), a double amputee exclaims, 'What scramble there'll be for arms and legs, when we old boys come out of our graves, on the Judgment Day: wonder if we shall get our own again? If we do, my leg will have to tramp from Fredericksburg, my arm from here, I suppose, and meet my body, wher-ever it may be' (ed. Showalter 1988, 25).

The desire for corporeal integrity and the fulfilling union of soma with brain/mind/psyche/soul goes back far in the past and, one confidently can predict, will continue long into the future. Miracles seem in short supply, immortality no longer broods, and we lack a covenant with the dead; modern medicine's covenant is with the living. The areligious demands of phantom pains and pleasures are being addressed by the many researchers and medical practi-tioners who, thankfully, are now on the case, in light of what a contemporary professor of neurology has described as a 'Copernican revolution' in the understanding of the relationship between the brain and the body (Halligan 2002, 253). Yet incomprehension of the type exemplified above persists, and much remains to be done. New issues keep arising – medical, moral, political.

The attention paid to PLS has diverted attention away from other brain-body communication issues – for example, functional neurological disorder (FND), formerly known as hysteria, to which it is very closely related. Indeed, FND, which involves limb weakness or paralysis (fixed dystonia) and dissociative or non-epileptic attacks, can be termed 'the opposite of PLS: your brain thinks your leg isn't there even though it is' (Jon Stone, personal communication). This has been seen predominantly, if not exclusively, as a mental rather than a brain issue (and referred to as 'body integrity identity disorder', or BIID, in the

---

[53] On the attitudes and rituals associated with the burial of limbs at this time, see Price 1976. More generally, there was concern that the spirit could not rest in peace if the body was in pieces. See Richardson 1988, 3–29, 75–99.

psychiatric literature), though there has been a movement to categorize it as a condition which requires neuroscientific investigation. Once again, suspicions of malingering have plagued research, but the suffering can be so extreme that some patients seek amputation. 'There is a paradoxical desire for self-repair through self-fragmentation' (Loewy 2020, 62); in order to feel whole, the patient wishes to lose a part of their existing body.[54]

The ethical implications alone are staggering. Bayne and Levy (2005) have gingerly explored the proposition that 'a limb that is not experienced as one's own is not in fact one's own', concluding that, if a patient experiencing BIID is enduring 'significant distress' to the extent that extreme self-harm or suicide is contemplated, then, providing 'no other effective treatment' is available, an operation 'might be permissible'. But the argument that surgery may be, *in extremis*, an effective therapy is weakened by the fact that some patients then seek further amputation. On the evidence of their own cases, Edwards, Carson & Stone (2011, 25) 'go so far as to say that … such a procedure would be unethical, as the chance of benefit is so low and the chance of significant harm so high'. The same conclusion is reached by Edwards et al. 2011, 1413: 'the outcome of amputation in fixed dystonia is invariably unfavorable'; 'symptoms typically return in the stump or another body part'. A patient could well exchange PIID suffering for PLP, one disorder in the central 'body schema' taking over from the other. All pain, no progress.[55]

Quite clearly and crucially, a lot depends on the degree of plasticity one allows the 'body schema'. Sometimes Ramachandran's prose struggles to express both aspects of the situation. At one point in his 1998 book, he remarks, 'For your entire life, you've been walking around assuming that your "self" is anchored to a single body that remains stable and permanent at least until death. Indeed, the "loyalty" of your self to your own body is so axiomatic that you never even pause to think about it, let alone question it'. And yet, he continues, certain simple experiments he has carried out (he has particularly in mind his mirror box therapy) 'suggest the exact opposite' – that your body schema, 'despite its appearance of durability, is an entirely transitory internal

---

[54] See Stone et al. 2005; Stone et al. 2010; Edwards et al. 2011; Nielsen et al. 2013; Edwards et al. 2014; Brugger & Christen 2016; Hansen et al. 2020. Loewy 2020 brings together ways in which PLS and BIID both 'involve a feeling of rupture underlined by a desire for wholeness' (i), considering material from literature, film and psychoanalysis.

[55] This Element has focused on phantom *limb* syndrome, not addressing the cultural significance of the reconstruction of the face, that crucial means of recognition and mark of individuality. The facial disfigurement of men returning from the two world wars of the twentieth century often meant social isolation, broken relationships and diminished job prospects. On the role of reconstructive plastic surgery, see Mayhew 2004, Meikle 2013 and Bamji 2017. For a moving 'Memorial to the Forgotten Faces of World War One', see www.gold.ac.uk/news/forgotten-faces -memorial/.

construct' (Ramachandran & Blakeslee 1998, 61–2). So, then, the 'body schema' is *both* quite stable *and* transitory? One can understand Ramachandran's wish to assert that some aspects of the 'body schema' are 'remappable', but here his rhetoric rather undermines other crucial aspects of his theory. Yet the compelling thought remains: a temporary creation can be re-created, can adapt to and indeed embrace, new physical circumstances, changes to the body's configuration (or, rather, the bodily configuration the brain started out with), whether people are born without certain body parts or lose them through accident or design.

The tensions coming into view here could well be placed within a chapter in the *longue durée* of the conflict between universalism/essentialism and social constructionism/relativism, which itself may be seen as part of a larger 'nature versus nurture' debate (fundamental distinctions well described by Plamper 2015). But the matter has its own rich complications. For a start, social constructionism has (in many of its most significant interventions) tended to privilege the collective over the individual, its relativism not being relative enough. Besides, the battle in question is being waged within neurology itself, or at least within the emergent movements of social neuroscience and critical neuroscience. One trend in neurology has affirmed that neurons are as unique as we are, thus allowing plenty of room for the particularities of individual identity. Another has insisted on an innately hard-wired 'body schema', as when Mulder et al. (2008) talk of 'a basic neural representation of the body that is, at least, partly genetically determined and by this relatively insensitive for changes in the sensory input' (1266). Or when Abramson and Feibel (1981) contend that 'a structural basis for the phantom experience is encoded in the DNA. We are born with a full-blown potential for imaging body parts' (99), those parts constituting and privileging a complete body (see Melzack 1990 and Melzack et al. 1997). Mezue & Makin 2017 have written powerfully of 'the immutability' of 'the brain's body representation' (43), while Muret & Makin (forthcoming) emphasize 'the brain's need for stability'. In the case of PLS, affirm Makin & Bensmaia 2017, 'the cortical representation of the limb remains remarkably stable despite the loss of its main peripheral input' (195).

Insofar as such claims tend towards universalism, they might be seen as opening the door for a version of neuromatrix determinism, selfhood being too easily and simplistically conflated with the biological brain. Troubling questions have been asked about the neuroscientific creation of the 'cerebral subject', defined as 'an anthropological figure that embodies the belief that human beings are essentially reducible to their brains' (Ortega & Vidal 2007, 255). On this formula, 'the brain is the only part of the body we need in order to be ourselves' (256), personhood being rendered identical with 'brainhood'. To express the matter provocatively, some neurologists may have come up with a theory of predestination which offers a potent replacement for a doctrine that generations of theologians have argued about.

Against which there have been many pushbacks. 'We are not reducible to the neuron', Crawford declares, going on to make the charming remark that 'on some days, I feel like *much more* than what my neurons are up to' (Crawford 2014, 232). And we may recall the resonant words of George Dedlow: 'a man is not his brain, or any one part of it, but all of his economy, and ... to lose any part must lessen this sense of his own existence' (Mitchell 1900, 139). Belief in the brain-as -self as 'a material system, governed by physical laws, and thus both morally innocent and robustly predictable' has encouraged a view of the neurostructural self as 'fixed and immutable', not open to 'intervention and optimization'. Here I am quoting Elizabeth Fein, who envisages the emergence of a firm division between medical conditions that are 'neurochemical', i.e. 'malleable, fluid, discovered by a psychiatry deeply reliant on psychopharmacology and amenable to its interventions', and those that are 'neurostructural', i.e. 'fixed and 'unfixable', intrinsic to personhood'. However, Fein suppresses the force of this troubling claim (an instance of narrative prosthesis?) by speaking of 'twin strands' of a single 'robust and consequential cultural model' which co-exist with each other, constituting 'a powerful and enduring complex of intertwined meanings' (Fein 2011, 27, 48). Others might find here an unbridgeable gap, or at least a tension which indicates the large amount of unfinished business facing medical researchers in many interweaving disciplines.

Medieval resurrection theory understood completeness in terms of the body and soul coming together, with all the body's parts also being reunited. No matter at what age a person had died, or how they had died, they would resurrect, quite intact, as mature adults; no matter if an individual had died as a baby (even as a fetus) or in extreme old age, his or her body would resurrect as it would have looked, or as it once had looked, at what was deemed the 'perfect age' of humankind's life (the age at which Christ had died). That theory has had a long and tenacious legacy, and, alongside notions surrounding the noble *imago Dei*, it has, I believe, helped define (for better or worse) some of the early parameters within which much psychosomatic research was conducted, encouraging attitudes which have lingered long into the present century. The model was of total reunification, with anyone who lacked limbs resurrecting whole, all blemishes and malformations excised; here was true personhood. If phantom limb sensation is placed within this conceptual framework, it is rendered quite unproblematic – here is an expression of desire for the return of a limb, a body part which shall be restored at the Resurrection. Body dysmorphic disorder (BDD), characterized by the obsessive idea that some aspect of one's own body part or appearance is severely flawed, would vanish instantly, given the beautiful perfection of the resurrected body – assuming that one belonged among the Blessed. One might continue the present fantasy with the thought that Body Integrity Identity Disorder (BIID), whereby the presence of an existing limb makes its owner (quite paradoxically) feel incomplete and therefore longs for its removal, would be a concept alien to the point of incomprehension – and quite horrifying to Dante's eagerly body-weaving phantoms.

Today, the question must be posed afresh, is an entire body necessary for personhood? If the brain contains and asserts a 'body schema' that presupposes and privileges a whole body, does this assume a sort of organic determinism, which maps out an inevitable destiny for both body and mind? Here one may suspect a troubling ableism, which is deep-seated even in progressive technologies. At present, the prosthetics industry offers not just freedom from some perceived physical lack but transcendence: its ingenious devices are not mere replacements for lost limbs but augmentations of what was there before, improvements on an original design which had faults and flaws.[56] These products are hyped with the promise of 'technologically achieved corporeal enhancement, self-actualization, aesthetic individuation, moral transcendence, and much more' (Crawford 2014, 3). But, is a missing body part indeed an impoverishment that must be remedied, or even bettered, by prosthesis, lest amputees are doomed to a psychic life of incompleteness, destined to feel, with George Dedlow, 'a deficiency in the egoistic sentiment of individuality' (Mitchell 1900, 138)?

---

[56] Beyond the discourse of replacement, compensation and restoration of functionality has developed one of enhancement and improvement: modern technology can provide artificial limbs which perform far better than the originals, thereby transcending the limitations and vulnerabilities of the weak human body. This has become a major motif in recent science fiction. An early, and highly successful, example was the TV series *The Six Million Dollar Man*, which ran from 1973 to 1978, spawning spin-off movies and the series *The Bionic Woman*. A former astronaut who, having been severely injured in an air crash, is rebuilt in a pioneering operation costing six million dollars. His right arm, both legs and left eye are replaced with bionic implants that greatly enhance his strength, speed and vision. The original program's tagline, 'We can rebuild him; we have the technology', became a popular 1970s catch-phrase. Its story-line was based on Martin Caidin's novel *Cyborg* (1972). That titular term had been in use since 1960, in referring to 'A person whose physical tolerances or capabilities are extended beyond normal human limitations by a machine or other external agency that modifies the body's functioning; an integrated man–machine system' (*OED* s.v. cyborg). The notion of extension of traditionally-defined tolerances or capabilities was powerfully developed in that masterpiece of feminist posthumanist theory, Donna Haraway's 'Cyborg Manifesto'. Here the interrelation of fiction and lived experience represented by the image of the cyborg, its boundary-shifting hybrid of machine-part and organism, prompts a radical call to social action: a reconstruction of 'the boundaries of daily life, in partial connection with others, in communication with all of our parts', which will effect 'a way out of the maze of dualisms in which we have explained our bodies and our tools to ourselves' (Haraway 1991).

I would hope not. And that hope is well-grounded in much current neuroscientific research. We may return to those statements that recognize and indeed celebrate the plasticity of the human brain, the large measure of adaptability and flexibility which is possible within it. 'Plasticity' is, one might say, the golden word that guards against charges of predestination and defends against accusations of neuroessentialism. We have already noted the vision of a 'body schema' that is 'relatively insensitive for changes in the sensory input' as put forward by Mulder et al. (2008). Yet they also declare that 'the adult human brain is not a rigid system but a system that continuously undergoes plastic changes after alterations in the sensory flow from peripheral receptors and nerve fibers' (1267). Tamar Makin, who (as quoted previously) has co-authored declarations of the immutability of the brain's body representation, its powerful need for stability, is an eloquent exponent of the organ's plasticity. Her 2013 essay on the relationship between deprivation-related and use-dependent plasticity demonstrates 'how experience-driven plasticity in the human brain can transcend boundaries that have been thought to limit reorganisation after sensory deprivation in adults' (Makin, Cramer et al. 2013). This study offers 'the first evidence that altered patterns of adaptive limb use, in individuals with unilateral hand absence, are reflected in distinct patterns of cortical reorganization', a conclusion supported by Hahamy et al. 2015, who demonstrate that 'whichever body part is being over-used to compensate for the absence of a hand also gains increased representation in the cortical territory of the missing hand'. Previously, research conducted by Borsook's team had indicated that somatosensory pathways in humans can rapidly reorganize, indeed within twenty-four hours (Borsook et al. 1998). It seems that the immutable body representation can change quickly when it wants to.

Given such moves into functional neuro-dynamics and neuro-plasticity, De Preester and Knockaert have the confidence to declare that 'neuronal determinism is no longer a plausible point of view'. Rather, 'a dynamic account is far more suitable for the phenomena at issue', and by adopting it neuroscience ceases to be 'imprisoned in the paradigm of the mechanical brain'. Insofar as they suggest rigidity, the Penfield homunculus and body 'maps' are no longer appropriate or adequate (De Preester & Knockaert 2005, 12). A major shift is being pronounced here, though it should be emphasized that some neuroscientists continue to regard the notions of the homunculus and body 'maps' as heuristically useful (see for instance Crick & Koch 2000 and Muret & Makin forthcoming).

A factor of historical progression must be recognised in the research. During the 1990s the hard-wired 'body schema' was big news, but recent research has become more aware of the wonderful plasticity which that schema can accommodate. That may be affirmed whilst recognizing that, in PLP, the brain's plasticity has not stretched far enough,[57] while in the case of FND it has stretched too far, overreached itself. In 2021, then, we can place emphasis on the fact that 'the neuromatrix is rapidly malleable/adaptable and greatly affected by visual representations and somatosensory stimuli' (Collins et al. 2018, 2169).[58] This supports the proposition that life – the life of an individual – is ongoingly inscribed into that individual's brain. 'No longer can we treat the brain as a bastion of unchanging nature' (Plamper 2015, 247).

* * *

Eighty-six billion neurons are said to be firing in the human brain. And yet, as Crick and Koch have emphasized, [O]ur subjective world of qualia – what distinguishes us from zombies and fills our life with color, music, smells, and other vivid sensations – is possibly caused by the activity of a small fraction of all the neurons in the brain, located strategically between the outer and the inner worlds. How these act to produce the subjective world that is so dear to us is still a complete mystery. (Crick & Koch 2000, 109)

Thanks to that small but vital fraction, in the human brain there is at once immutability and mutability, stability and plasticity, resistance to change yet lack of rigidity: such is its complex nature. As Peter Brugger has nicely put it (in a personal communication), the brain's body representations have a *dynamic stability.*

The 'body schema' is always with us, and stable in that sense; quite reliable and with us until we die (Augustine and Dante would say that it continues beyond death). We can be confident of that. However, certain specific changes are possible; at least parts of the brain have a remarkable dynamism and ability to adapt. Hence, that same schema can be described, albeit with some rhetorical exaggeration, as 'merely a shell that you've temporarily created for successfully passing on your genes to your offspring' (Ramachandran & Blakeslee 1998, 62). A temporary creation can be re-created, replaced with a new one which challenges standard notions of the missing, the lacking, the deficient and the inadequate, without hindering our genes' routes of passage or being hampered by them.

Through this re-creation, in the lives of patients and in the research of the professionals who treat them, pain may be better understood and better relieved. 'Pain is, above all, an elaborate expression of the workings of the brain'

---

[57] See especially Flor et al. 2006, for a discussion of whether PLP may be seen as 'a case of maladaptive CNS plasticity'. Mezue & Makin 2017 take a very positive line, arguing that brain plasticity following amputation is assistive and supportive rather than maladaptive.

[58] See further Botvinick & Cohen 1998; McCabe et al. 2005; and Ehrsson 2007.

(Cervero & Jensen 2006, vii); the more we learn about the brain, the more we learn about pain, and vice versa. Stable knowledge of the mysterious organ which produces our subjective world is the ultimate Holy Grail of neuroscience. Which remains elusive, glimpsed but not yet fully seen.

> 'I heard the sound, I saw the light,
> But since I did not see the Holy Thing,
> I sware a vow to follow it till I saw.'
> (Tennyson, 'The Holy Grail'; Camelot Project)[59]

---

[59] The speaker is a grail-knight, Sir Percivale.

References

Abramson, A. S., & Feibel, A. (1981). The phantom phenomenon: Its use and disuse. *Bulletin of the New York Academy of Medicine*, 57, 99–112.

Algioti, S. A., Cortese, F., & Franchini, C. (1994). Rapid sensory remapping in the adult human brain as inferred from phantom breast perception. *Neuroreport*, 5(4), 473–6.

Andoh, J., Diers, M., Milde, C., et al. (2017). Neural correlates of evoked phantom limb sensations. *Biological Psychology*, 126, 89–97.

Aquinas, Thomas (1964–81). *Summa theologiae*, Blackfriars edition, 61 vols. London and New York: Eyre and Spottiswoode.

Arcadi, J. A. (1977). Phantom bladder: Is this an unusual entity? *Journal of Urology*, 118, 354–5.

Aternali, Andrea, & Katz, Joel. (2019). Recent advances in understanding and managing phantom limb pain. *F1000Research*, 8, 1167.

Bamji, Andrew. (2017). *Faces from the Front: Harold Gillies, the Queen's Hospital, Sidcup and the Origins of Modern Plastic Surgery*. Solihull, West Midlands: Helion & Company.

Barbezat, M. D. (2013). In a corporeal flame: The materiality of hellfire before the Resurrection in six Latin authors. *Viator*, 44, 1–20.

Barney, Stephen A., et al., eds. (2006). *The Etymologies of Isidore of Seville*. Cambridge: Cambridge University Press.

Bartlett, Robert. (2013). *Why Can the Dead Do Such Great Things?: Saints and Worshippers from the Martyrs to the Reformation*. Princeton: Princeton University Press.

Bekrater-Bodmann, Robin. (2016). The phantoms in our dreams. *Relief: Pain Research News, Insights and Ideas*, September 29, https://relief.news/phantom-limb-pain-body-representation-dreams/.

Berlucchi, Giovanni, & Aglioti, Salvatore. (1997). The 'body in the brain': The neural bases of corporeal awareness. *Trends in Neurosciences*, 20, 560–4.

Berlucchi, Giovanni, & Aglioti, Salvatore M. (2010). The body in the brain revisited. *Experimental Brain Research*, 200, 25–35.

Blakeslee, Sandra. (2006). Out-of-body experience? Your brain is to blame. *New York Times*, October 3, www.nytimes.com/2006/10/03/health/psychology/03shad.html.

Blanke, Olaf, & Mohr, Christine. (2005). Out-of-body experience, heautoscopy, and autoscopic hallucination of neurological origin: Implications for neurocognitive mechanisms of corporeal awareness and self consciousness. *Brain Research Reviews*, 50, 184–99.

Boddice, Rob (2017). *Pain: A Very Short Introduction*. Oxford: Oxford University Press.

Borsook, D., Becerra, L., Fishman, S., et al. (1998). Acute plasticity in the human somatosensory cortex following amputation. *Neuroreport*, 9(6), 1013–17.

Botterill, Steven. (1994). *Dante and the Mystical Tradition: Bernard of Clairvaux in the 'Commedia'*. Cambridge: Cambridge University Press.

Botvinick, M., & Cohen, J. (1998). Rubber hands 'feel' touch that eyes see. *Nature*, 391(6669), 756.

Bourke, Joanna. (2014a). Phantom suffering: Amputees, stump pain and phantom sensations in modern Britain. In Boddice, Rob, ed., *Pain and Emotion in Modern History*. Houndmills, Basingstoke: Palgrave Macmillan, 66–89.

Bourke, Joanna. (2014b). *The Story of Pain: From Prayer to Painkillers*. Oxford: Oxford University Press.

Boxall, Peter. (2020). *The Prosthetic Imagination: A History of the Novel as Artificial Life*. Cambridge: Cambridge University Press.

Brain, Walter Russell. (1941). Visual distortion with special reference to the regions of the right hemisphere. *Brain*, 64, 244–72.

Bressler, Steven L., & Menon, Vinod. (2010). Large-scale brain networks in cognition: Emerging methods and principles. *Trends in Cognitive Sciences*, 14, 277–90.

Brooke-Rose, Christine. (1970). The foot. In *Go When You See the Green Man Walking*. London: Michael Joseph, 43–64.

Brugger, Peter. (2006). From phantom limb to phantom body. In Knoblich Günther, Thornton, Ian K., et. al. eds., *Human Body Perception from the Inside Out*. Oxford: Oxford University Press, 171–209.

Brugger, Peter. (2008). The phantom limb in dreams. *Consciousness and Cognition*, 17, 1272–8.

Brugger, Peter. (2012). Tabula Rama: Review of Ramachandran, V. S. *Cognitive Neuropsychiatry*, 17(4), 351–8.

Brugger, Peter. (2013). Autoscopic phenomena. In Pashler Harold, ed., *Encyclopedia of the Mind*, 2 vols. Los Angeles & London: Sage Reference, I, 99–102.

Brugger, Peter. (2015). Phenomenology of phantomology: Lessons from epilepsy, for the Third International Congress on epilepsy, brain, and mind: Part 2, at www.zora.uzh.ch/id/eprint/115491/1/Rector%20et%20al.%202015%20Epilepsy%20%26%20Behavior%20%28part%20Brugger%3B%20for%20ZORA.pdf. See also Brugger (no date given), Phantomology: The Science of the Body in the Brain, at Artbrain.org, www.artbrain.org/phantomology-the-science-of-the-body-in-the-brain/.

Brugger, Peter, Christen, Markus, et al. (2016). Limb amputation and other disability desires as a medical condition. *Lancet Psychiatry*, 3(12), 1176–86.

Brugger, Peter, & Funk, Marion. (2007). Out on a limb, neglect and confabulation in the study of aplasic phantoms. In Della Sala, Sergio, ed., *Tall Tales about the Mind and Brain: Separating Fact from Fiction*. Oxford: Oxford University Press, 348–68.

Brugger, Peter, Kollias, Spyros S., Müri, René M., et al. (2000). Beyond re-membering: Phantom sensations of congenitally absent limbs. *Proceedings of the National Academy of Sciences of the United States of America*, 97(11), 6167–72.

Brugger, Peter, & Mohr, Christine. (2009). Out of the body, but not out of mind. *Cortex*, 45, 137–40.

Brugger, P., Regard, M., & Landis, T. (1997). Illusory reduplication of one's own body: phenomenology and classification of autoscopic phenomena. *Cognitive Neuropsychiatry*, 7, 179–94.

Burrow, J. A. (1986). *The Ages of Man: A Study in Medieval Writing and Thought*. Oxford: Clarendon Press.

Bynum, Caroline Walker. (2017). *The Resurrection of the Body in Western Christianity, 200–1336*. New York: Columbia University Press.

Caesarius, ed. Aloys Meister. (1901). *Die fragmente der Libri VIII miraculorum des Caesarius von Heisterbach*. Römische Quartalschrift für christliche Alterthumskunde und für Kirkengeschichte, suppl. 13. Rom: Spithöver.

Camelot Project. Alfred Lord Tennyson, 'Idylls of the King' (1859–85), at https://d.lib.rochester.edu/camelot/text/tennyson-the-holy-grail.

Cervero, Fernando, & Jensen, Troels S. (2006). Preface. In *Pain: Handbook of Clinical Neurology*, 3rd srs, vol. 3. Edinburgh & New York: Elsevier, vii–viii.

Cervetti, Nancy. (2012). *S. Weir Mitchell, 1829–1914: Philadelphia's Literary Physician*. University Park, PA: Penn State University Press.

Cheyne, J. Allan, & Girard, Todd A. (2009). The body unbound: vestibular-motor hallucinations and out-of-body experiences. *Cortex*, 45(2), 201–15.

Chiamenti, Massimiliano, ed. (2002). Pietro Alighieri, *Comentum super poema Comedie Dantis: A Critical Edition of the Third and Final Draft of Pietro Alighieri's Commentary on Dante's 'Divine Comedy'*. Tempe, AZ. Accessed through the Dartmouth Dante Project, at https://dante.dartmouth.edu/.

Cipriani, Gabriele, Picchi, Lucia, et al. (2011). The phantom and the supernumerary phantom limb: Historical review and new case. *Neuroscience Bulletin*, 27, 359–65.

Collins, Kassondra L., Russell, Hannah, G., Schumacher, Patrick J., et al. (2018). A review of current theories and treatments for phantom limb pain. *Journal of Clinical Investigation*, 128(6), 2168–76.

Crawford, Cassandra S. (2014). *Phantom Limb. Amputation, Embodiment, and Prosthetic Technology*. New York: NYU Press.

Crick, Francis, & Koch, Christof. (2000). The Unconscious Homunculus. In Metzinger, ed., *Neural Correlates of Consciousness*, 103–10.

Critchley, M. (1979). Corporeal awareness: Body image; body scheme. In Critchley, M., ed., *The Divine Banquet of the Brain*. Raven Press: New York, 92–105.

De Preester, Helena, & Knockaert, Veroniek, eds. (2005). *Body image and body schema, interdisciplinary perspectives on the body*. Amsterdam & Philadelphia: Benjamins.

Dening, T. R., & Berrois, G. E. (1994). Autoscopic phenomena. *British Journal of Psychiatry*, 165(6), 808–17.

DMLBS. Dictionary of Medieval Latin from British Sources, online version, at https://logeion.uchicago.edu.

Dyson, R. W. (1998), tr. Augustine, *De civitate Dei*. Cambridge: Cambridge University Press.

Edwards, Mark J., Alonso-Canovas, Araceli, Schrag, Arnette, et al. (2011). Limb amputations in fixed dystonia: A form of body integrity identity disorder? *Movement Disorders*, 26(8), 1410–14.

Edwards, M. J., Stone, J., & Lang, A. E. (2014). From psychogenic movement disorder to functional movement disorder: It's time to change the name. *Movement Disorders*, 29(7), 849–52.

Edwards, Mark J., Carson, Alan, & Stone, Jon. (2011). To amputate or not: A conundrum in fixed dystonia with complex regional pain. *ACNR (Advances in Clinical Neuroscience and Rehabilitation)*, 11(2), 22–5.

Ehrsson, H. H. (2007). The experimental induction of out-of-body experiences. *Science*, 317(5841), 1048.

Elliott, Dyan. (1999). *Fallen Bodies: Pollution, Sexuality, and Demonology in the Middle Ages*. Philadelphia: University of Pennsylvania Press.

Fein, Elizabeth. (2011). Innocent machines: Asperger's syndrome and the neurostructural self. In Pickersgill, M., & Van Keulen, I, eds., *Sociological Reflections on the Neurosciences*: Bingley: Emerald Group Publications, 27–49.

Finger, Stanley, & Hustwit, Meredith. (2003). Five early accounts of phantom limb in context: Paré, Descartes, Lemos, Bell, and Mitchell. *Neurosurgery*, 52, 675–86.

Fisher, J. P., Hassan, D. T., & O'Connor, N. (1995). *British Medical Journal*, 310, 70. Accessed at https://doi.org/10.1136/bmj.310.6971.70.

Flor, Herta. (2002). Phantom limb pain: Characteristics, causes, and treatment. *The Lancet Neurology*, 1(3), 182–9.

Flor, Herta, Nikolajsen, Lone, & Jensen, Troels Staehelin. (2006). Phantom limb pain: A case of maladaptive CNS plasticity? *Neuroscience*, 7, 873–81.

Funk, Marion, Shiffrar, Maggie, & Brugger, Peter. (2005). Hand movement observation by individuals born without hands: Phantom limb experience constrains visual limb perception. *Experimental Brain Research*, 164, 341–6.

Glare, P. G. W., ed. (2012). *Oxford Latin Dictionary*, 2nd ed., 2 vols. Oxford: Oxford University Press.

Goodich, Michael. (2007). *Miracles and Wonders. The Development of the Concept of Miracle, 1150–1350*. Aldershot: Ashgate.

Grottaferrata, eds. (1971–81). *Sententiae in IV libris distinctae*, Spicilegium Bonaventurianum, 4–5, 2 vols. Grottaferrata: Editiones Collegii S. Bonaventurae ad Claras Aquas.

Grüsser, S. M., Mühlnickel, W., Schaefer, M., et al. (2004). Remote activation of referred phantom sensation and cortical reorganization in human upper extremity amputees. *Experimental Brain Research*, 154, 97–102.

Guenther, Katja. (2016). 'It's All Done With Mirrors': V. S. Ramachandran and the Material Culture of Phantom Limb Research. *Medical History*, 60(3), 342–58.

Haggard, P., & Wolpert, D. M. (2005). Disorders of body scheme. In Freund, Hans-Joachim, Jeannerod, Marc, Hallett, Mark, & Leiguarda, Ramon. *Higher-Order Motor Disorders. From Neuroanatomy and Neurobiology to Clinical Neurology*. Oxford: Oxford University Press, 261–71.

Hahamy, Avital, Sotiropoulos, Stamatios N., Slater, David Henderson, et al. (2015). Normalisation of brain connectivity through compensatory behaviour, despite congenital hand absence. *eLife*, 4:e04605.

Hallett, Mark, Stone, Jon, & Carson, Alan, eds. (2016). *Functional neurologic disorders. Handbook of Clinical Neurology*, 3rd series. Amsterdam: Elsevier.

Halligan, Peter W. (2002). Phantom limbs: The body in mind. *Cognitive Neuropsychiatry*, 7(3), 251–68.

Haraway, Donna. (1991). A cyborg manifesto: Science, technology, and socialist-feminism in the late twentieth century. In Haraway, Donna, *Simians, Cyborgs and Women: The Reinvention of Nature*. New York: Routledge, 149–81.

Head, Henry. (1918). Sensation and the cerebral cortex. *Brain*, 41, 57–123.

Head, Henry. (1919). *'Destroyers' and Other Verses*. London: Oxford University Press.

Head, H., & Holmes, G. (1911). Sensory disturbances from cerebral lesions. *Brain*, 34(2–3), 102–254.

Herrmann, B., & Gibbs, W. (1945). Phantom limb pain: Its relation to the treatment of large nerves at the time of amputation. *American Journal of Surgery*, 67, 168–80.

Herschbach, Lisa. (1995). 'True clinical fictions': Medical and literary narratives from the Civil War hospital. *Culture, Medicine and Psychiatry*, 19 (1995), 183–205.

Herschbach, Lisa. (1997). Prosthetic reconstructions: Making the industry, re-making the body, modelling the nation. *History Workshop Journal*, 44, 22–57.

Hill, Edmund, tr. (2002). *Augustine: On Genesis. The Works of Saint Augustine: A Translation for the 21st Century*, 1(13). New York: New City Press.

Hill, Edmund, tr. (2005). *Augustine, De divinatione daemonum, in Augustine: On Christian Belief. The Works of Saint Augustine: A Translation for the 21st Century*, 1(8). New York: New City Press.

Hoffman, Julius. (1954). Phantom limb syndrome: A critical review of literature. *Journal of Nervous and Mental Disease*, 119, 261–70.

Holland, Henry Richard (1852–4). *Memoirs of the Whig Party during my time, by Henry Richard Lord Holland, edited by his son, Henry Edward Lord Holland*. London: Longman.

Ingraham (2020). Pain is weird: A volatile, misleading sensation. *Pain Science*, updated 27 February 2020, accessed www.painscience.com/articles/pain-is-weird.php.

Jarrett, Christian. (2012). Mirror neurons: The most hyped concept in neuroscience? Mirror neurons are fascinating but they aren't the answer to what makes us human. *Psychology Today* (10 December 2012), at www.psychologytoday.com/gb/blog/brain-myths/201212/mirror-neurons-the-most-hyped-concept-in-neuroscience.

Jarrett, Christian. (2013). A calm look at the most hyped concept in neuroscience: Mirror neurons. *Wired*, 12, at www.wired.com/2013/12/a-calm-look-at-the-most-hyped-concept-in-neuroscience-mirror-neurons/.

Katz, J., & Melzack, R. (1990). Pain 'memories' in phantom limbs: Review and clinical observations. *Pain*, 43(3), 319–36.

Kelham, R. D. Langdale (1952). *Artificial Limbs in the Rehabilitation of the Disabled*. London: HMSO, 1952.

Kilner, J. M., & Lemon, R. N. (2013). What we know currently about mirror neurons. *Current Biology*, 23(23), 1057–62.

Knecht, S., Henningsen, H., Elbert, T., et al. (1996). Reorganizational and perceptional changes after amputation. *Brain*, 119, 1213–19.

Laqueur, Thomas W. (2015). *The Work of the Dead: A Cultural History of Mortal Remains*. Princeton: Princeton University Press.

Loewy, Monika. (2020). *Phantom Limbs and Body Integrity Identity Disorder. Literary and Psychoanalytic Perspectives*. London & New York: Routledge.

Luibheid, Colm, tr. (1987). *Pseudo-Dionysius: The Complete Works*: New York and Mahwah, NJ: Paulist Press.

Makin, Tamar R., & Bensmaia, Sliman J. (2017). Stability of sensory topographies in adult cortex. *Trends in Cognitive Sciences*, 21(3), 195–204.

Makin, Tamar R., Cramer, Alona O., Scholz, Jan, et al. (2013). Deprivation-related and use-dependent plasticity go hand in hand. *eLife*, 2:e01273.

Matthews, Gareth B. (2015). Death in Socrates, Plato and Aristotle. In Bradley, Ben, & Feldman, Fred, eds., *The Oxford Handbook of Philosophy of Death*. Oxford: Oxford University Press, 186–99.

Mayhew, Emily R. (2004). *The Reconstruction of Warriors: Archibald McIndoe, the Royal Air Force and the Guinea Pig Club*. London: Greenhill.

McCabe, C. S., Haigh, R. C., Halligan, P. W., & Blake, D. R. (2005). Simulating sensory-motor incongruence in healthy volunteers: Implications for a cortical model of pain. *Rheumatology (Oxford)*, 44(4), 509–16.

McGinn, Bernard, ed. (1977). *Three Treatises on Man: A Cistercian Anthropology*. Kalamazoo, MI: Cistercian Publications.

Meikle, Murray C. (2013). *Reconstructing Faces: The Art and Wartime Surgery of Gillies, Pickerill, McIndoe and Mowlem*. Dunedin: Otago University Press.

Melzack, Ronald. (1989). Phantom limbs, the self, and the brain. *Canadian Psychology/Psychologie Canadienne*, 30, 1–16.

Melzack, Ronald. (1990). Phantom limbs and the concept of a neuromatrix. *Trends in Neurosciences*, 13, 88–92.

Melzack, Ronald. (1992). Phantom limbs. *Scientific American*, 266(4), 120–6.

Melzack, Ronald et al. (1997). Phantom limbs in people with congenital limb deficiency or amputation in early childhood. *Brain*, 120, 1603–20.

Merzenich, M. M., Kaas, J. H., Wall, J., et al. (1983). Topographic reorganization of somatosensory cortical areas 3b and 1 in adult monkeys following restricted deafferentation. *Neuroscience*, 8(1), 33–55.

Metzinger, Thomas, ed. (2000). *Neural Correlates of Consciousness: Empirical and Conceptual Questions*. Cambridge, MA: The MIT Press.

Metzinger, Thomas. (2000). The subjectivity of subjective experience: A representationalist analysis of the first-person perspective. In Metzinger, ed., *Neural Correlates of Consciousness*, 285–306.

Metzinger, Thomas. (2004). *Being No One. The Self-Model Theory of Subjectivity*, 2nd ed. Cambridge, MA: The MIT Press.

Metzinger, Thomas. (2005). Out-of-body experiences as the origin of the concept of a 'soul'. *Mind & Matter*, 3(1), 57–84.

Metzinger, Thomas. (2009). Why are out-of-body experiences interesting for philosophers? The theoretical relevance of OBE research. *Cortex*, 45, 256–8.

Metzler, Irina. (2006). *Disability in Medieval Europe: Thinking about Physical Impairment during the High Middle Ages, c. 1100–1400*. London & New York: Routledge.

Metzler, Irina. (2016). *Fools and Idiots? Intellectual Disability in the Middle Ages*. Manchester: Manchester University Press.

Mews, Constant. (2018). Debating the authority of Pseudo-Augustine's *De spiritu et anima*. *Przegląd Tomistyczny*, 24, 321–48.

Mezue, Melvin, & Makin, Tamar. (2017). Immutable body representations: Lessons from phantoms in amputees. In de Vignemont, Frederique, & Alsmith, Adrian J. T., *The Subject's Matter: Self-Consciousness and the Body*. Cambridge, MA: The MIT Press: 33–50.

Minnis, Alastair. (2016). *From Eden to Eternity: Creations of Paradise in the Later Middle Ages*. Philadelphia: University of Pennsylvania Press.

Minnis, Alastair. (2020). *Hellish Imaginations from Augustine to Dante: An Essay in Metaphor and Materiality*. Oxford: Society for the Study of Medieval Languages and Literature.

Miracles, ed. Warner (1885). *Miracles de Nostre Dame*, ed. George Warner. Westminster: Nichols.

Mitchell, S. Weir. (1871). Phantom limbs. *Lippincott's Magazine of Popular Literature and Science*, 8(48), 563–9.

Mitchell, S. Weir. (1872). *Injuries of Nerves and Their Consequences*. Philadelphia: Lippincott.

Mitchell, S. Weir. (1883). *The Hill of Stones and Other Poems*. Boston: Houghton, Mifflin and Co.

Mitchell, S. Weir. (1900). *The Autobiography of a Quack and The Case of George Dedlow*, illustrated by A. J. Keller. New York: The Century Co.

Mitchell, David, & Snyder, Sharon, eds. (2014). *Narrative Prosthesis: Disability and the Dependencies of Discourse*. Ann Arbor: University of Michigan Press.

Mowbray, Donald. (2009). *Pain and Suffering in Medieval Theology: Academic Debates at the University of Paris in the Thirteenth Century*. Woodbridge: Boydell & Brewer.

Mulder, T., Hochstenbach, J., Dijkstra, P. U., et al. (2008). Born to adapt, but not in your dreams. *Consciousness and Cognition*, 17, 1266–71.

Muret, Dollyanne, & Makin, Tamar R. (forthcoming). The Homeostatic Homunculus: Rethinking Deprivation-Triggered Reorganization.

Nardi, Bruno. (1960). *Studi di filosofia medievale*. Rome, Edizioni di Storia e letteratura.

Newman, William R. (1999). The Homunculus and his forbears: Wonders of art and nature. In Grafton, Anthony, & Siraisi, Nancy, eds., *Natural Particulars: Nature and the Disciplines in Renaissance Europe*. Cambridge, MA: The MIT Press.

Newman, William R. (2004). *Promethean Ambitions: Alchemy and the Quest to Perfect Nature*. Chicago: University of Chicago Press.

Newman, Barbara, tr. (2017). *Mechthild of Hackeborn: The Book of Special Grace*. New York: Paulist Press.

Nielsen, G., Stone, J., & Edwards, M. J. (2013). Physiotherapy for functional (psychogenic) motor symptoms: A systematic review. *Journal of Psychosomatic Research*, 75(2), 93–102.

Nikolajsen, L., & Jensen, T. S. (2001). Phantom limb pain. *British Journal of Anaesthesia*, 87(1), 107–16.

O'Connor, Erin. (1997). 'Fractions of Men': Engendering Amputation in Victorian Culture. *Comparative Studies in Society and History*, 39(4), 742–77.

O'Sullivan, Suzanne. (2016). *It's All in Your Head: Stories from the Frontline of Psychosomatic Illness*. Reprint. London: Vintage.

OED. Oxford English Dictionary, online version. Accessed at www.oed.com/.

Oppenheim, Janet. (1985). *The Other World: Spiritualism and Psychical Research in England, 1850–1914*. Cambridge: Cambridge University Press.

Ortega, Francisco, & Vidal, Fernando. (2007). Mapping the cerebral subject in contemporary culture. *Electronic Journal of Communication, Innovation & Innovation in Health (Rio de Janeiro)*, 1(2), 255–9.

Osler, William. (1905). *Science and Immortality*, The 1904 Ingersoll Lecture, 6th impression. Boston & New York: Houghton, Mifflin & Company.

Paillard, J. (1975). Discussion du rapport de R. Angelergue sur 'Reflexions sur la notion de schéma corporel'. In *Symposium de l'APSLF (Paris, 1973): Psychologie de la conscience de soi*. Paris: Presses Universitaires de France, 143–8.

Paillard, J. (1999). Body schema and body image – a double dissociation in deafferented patients. In Gantchev, G. N., Mori. S., & Massion, J., eds. *Motor Control, Today and Tomorrow*. Sophia: Academic Publishing House, 197–214.

Paré, Ambroise. (1649). *The Workes of That Famous Chirurgion Ambrose Parey, Translated Out of Latine and Compared with the French, by Tho. Johnson*. London: Richard Cotes.

Penfield, Wilder, & Rasmussen, Theodore. (1950). *The Cerebral Cortex of Man: A Clinical Study of Localization of Function*. New York, Macmillan.

Perry, B. N., Moran, C. W., Armiger, R. S., et al. (2018). Initial clinical evaluation of the modular prosthetic limb. *Frontiers in Neurology*, 9, 153.

Petrocchi, Giorgio (1994), ed. Dante, *La Commedia secondo l'antica vulgate*. 4 vols., rev. reprint ed. Florence: Le Lettere.

Plamper, Jan. (2015). *The History of Emotions: An introduction*. Oxford: Oxford University Press.

Price, Douglas B. (1976). Miraculous restoration of lost body parts: Relationship to the phantom limb phenomenon and to limb-burial superstitions and practices. In Hand, Wayland D., ed., *American Folk Medicine: A Symposium*. Berkeley: University of California Press, 49–71.

Price, Douglas B., & Twombly, Neil J. (1978). *The Phantom Limb Phenomenon: A Medical, Folkloric, and Historical Study: Texts and Translations of 10th to 20th Century Accounts of the Miraculous Restoration of Lost Body Parts*. Washington, DC: Georgetown University Press.

Prothero, Stephen. (2002). *Purified by Fire: A History of Cremation in America*. Berkeley: University of California Press.

Quaracchi editors (1882–1902). *Bonaventurae opera omnia*, 11 vols. Quaracchi: Editiones Collegii S. Bonaventurae ad Claras Aquas.

Ramachandran, V. S. (2011). *The Tell-Tale Brain: A Neuroscientist's Quest for What Makes Us Human*. New York: W. W. Norton.

Ramachandran, V. S. (2012). Author response to review by Peter Brugger of *The Tell-Tale Brain* (2011). *Cognitive Neuropsychiatry*, 17(4), 359–66.

Ramachandran, V. S., & Blakeslee, Sandra. (1998). *Phantoms in the Brain: Human Nature and the Architecture of the Mind*. London and New York: HarperCollins.

Ramachandran, V. S., & Hirstein, William. (1998). The perception of phantom limbs. *Brain*, 121, 1603–30.

Ramachandran, V. S., & Rogers-Ramachandran, D. (2008). Sensations referred to a patient's phantom arm from another subject's intact arm: Perceptual correlates of mirror neurons. *Medical Hypotheses*, 70, 1233–4.

Regan, Richard, & Davies, Brian, eds. (2001). *The De Malo of Thomas Aquinas*. Oxford: Oxford University Press.

Richardson, Ruth. (1988). *Death, Dissection and the Destitute*. Harmondsworth: Penguin Books.

Riddoch, George. (1941). Phantom limbs and body shape. *Brain*, 64 (4), 197–222.

Rizzolatti, G., Camarda, R., Fogassi, L., et al. (1988). Functional organization of inferior area 6 in the macaque monkey. II. Area F5 and the control of distal movements. *Experimental Brain Research*, 71, 491–507.

Satz, Aura. (2010). 'The conviction of its existence': Silas Weir Mitchell, phantom limbs and phantom bodies in neurology and spiritualism. In Salisbury, L., & Shail, A., eds., *Neurology and Modernity: A Cultural History of Nervous Systems, 1800–1950*. New York: Palgrave Macmillan, 113–29.

Schilder, Paul. (1923, rpt. 2013). *Das Körperschema: Ein Beitrag zur Lehre vom Bewusstsein des Eigenen Körpers*. Berlin: Springer.

Schilder, Paul. (1935, rpt. 1999). *The Image and Appearance of the Human Body: Studies in the Constructive Energies of the Psyche*. New York: International Universities Press.

Schott, G. D. (1993). Penfield's homunculus: A note on cerebral cartography. *Journal of Neurology, Neurosurgery, and Psychiatry*, 56, 329–33.

Sherman, R. A., Sherman, C. J., & Parker, L. (1984). Chronic phantom and stump pain among American veterans: Results of a survey. *Pain*, 18(1), 83–95.

Silano, Giulio, tr. (2007–10). Peter Lombard, *Sententiae in IV libris distinctae*, 4 vols. Toronto: Pontifical Institute of Mediaeval Studies.

Simmel, Marianne L. (1956). On phantom limbs. *Archives of Neurology and Psychiatry*, 75, 637–47.

Singleton, Charles S., ed. and tr. (1977). Dante, *Comedy*, 3 vols, rev. reprint ed. Princeton: Princeton University Press.

Sobchack, Vivian. (2006). A leg to stand on: Prosthetics, metaphor, and materiality. In Smith, Marquard, & Morra, Johanne, eds., *The Prosthetic Impulse: From a Posthuman Present to a Biocultural Future*. Cambridge, MA: The MIT Press, 17–42.

Spicker, S. F. T. (1975). The lived body as catalytic agent: Reaction at the interface of medicine and philosophy. In Engelhardt, H. R., & Spicker, S. F., eds., *Evaluation and Explanation in the Biomedical Sciences*. Dordrecht: Reidel Publishing Co.: 181–204.

Stallings-Taney, M., ed. (1997). *Meditaciones vite Christi, olim Bonaventuro attributae*, Corpus Christianorum Continuatio Medievalis 153. Turnhout: Brepols.

Stamenov, Maxim. (2005). Body schema, body image, and mirror neurons. In De Preester & Knockaert, eds., *Body Image and Body Schema*, 21–43.

Stone, Jon, Carson, Alan, Duncan, R., et al. (2010). Who is referred to neurology clinics? – The diagnoses made in 3781 new patients. *Clinical Neurology and Neurosurgery*, 112(9), 747–51.

Stone, Jon, Smyth, Roger, Carson, Alan, et al. (2005). Systematic review of misdiagnosis of conversion symptoms and 'hysteria'. *British Medical Journal*, 331(7523), 989.

Tennyson, Alfred. (2007). *Tennyson: A Selected Edition*, ed. Christophei Ricks, rev. ed. London and New York: Routledge.

Teske, Ronald. (2001). Augustine's philosophy of memory. In Stump, Eleonore, & Kretzmann, Norman, eds., *The Cambridge Companion to Augustine*, 1st ed. Cambridge: Cambridge University Press, 148–58.

Thomas, Daniel L., & Thomas, Lucy B. (1920). *Kentucky Superstitions*. Princeton, NJ: Princeton University Press.

Thomson, Ian, & Perraud, Louis, tr. (1990). *Ten Latin Schooltexts of the Later Middle Ages*. Lewiston: Mellen.

Tóth, Peter, & Falway, Dâvid. (2014). New light on the date and authorship of the *Meditationes vitae Christi*. In Kelly, Stephen, & Perry, Ryan, eds., *Devotional Culture in Late Medieval England and Europe: Diverse Imaginations of Christ's Life*. Turnhout: Brepols, 17–105.

Wade, Nicholas J. (2003). The Legacy of Phantom Limbs. *Perception*, 32, 517–24.

Wade, Nicholas J. (2009). Beyond body experiences: Phantom limbs, pain and the locus of sensation. *Cortex*, 45, 243–55.

Weiss, S. A., & Fishman, S. (1963). Extended and telescoped phantom limbs in unilateral amputees. *Journal of Abnormal Social Psychology*, 66, 489–97.

White, P. D., Rickards, H., & Zeman, Adam. (2012). Time to end the distinction between mental and neurological illnesses. *British Medical Journal*, 344, e3454.

Whitney, Annie W., & Bullock, Caroline C. (1925). Folk-lore from Maryland. *Memoirs of the American Folklore Society*, 18. New York: American Folklore Society.

Woolgar, C. M. (2006). *The Senses in Late Medieval England*. New Haven, CT: Yale University Press.

Zeman, Adam. (2014). Neurology is psychiatry – and vice versa. *Practical Neurology*, 4, 136–44.

Acknowledgements

This essay began with a conversation with my daughter Dr Sarah Minnis-Lyons, a gastroenterologist working in Edinburgh, and so I happily dedicate it to her. I am particularly grateful to three neuroscientists who patiently answered my many queries: Peter Brugger (Professor of Behavioral Neurology and Neuropsychiatry at the University of Zurich), Jon Stone (NHS Consultant Neurologist and Honorary Professor of Neurology at Edinburgh University) and Tamar Makin (Professor of Cognitive Neuroscience at University College London). Flaws in understanding and presentation are totally mine. Among my medievalist friends and colleagues, I am particularly indebted to Ian Johnson, Gina Hurley and Andrew Kraebel for their support in an intellectual enterprise that took me beyond my usual comfort zone. Jan Plamper's editorial encouragement and input were transformative.

Cambridge Elements ⎓

Histories of Emotions and the Senses

Jan Plamper
Goldsmiths, University of London

Jan Plamper is Professor of History at Goldsmiths, University of London, where he teaches an MA seminar on the history of emotions. His publications include *The History of Emotions: An Introduction* (2015), a multidisciplinary volume on fear with contributors from neuroscience to horror film to the 1929 stock market crash, and articles on the sensory history of the Russian Revolution and the history of soldiers' fears in World War I. He has also authored *The Stalin Cult: A Study in the Alchemy of Power* (2012) and, in German, *The New We. Why Migration is No Problem: A Different History of the Germans* (2019).

About the Series
Born of the emotional and sensory 'turns', Elements in Histories of Emotions and the Senses move one of the fastest-growing interdisciplinary fields forward. The series is aimed at scholars across the humanities, social sciences, and life sciences, embracing insights from a diverse range of disciplines, from neuroscience to art history and economics. Chronologically and regionally broad, encompassing global, transnational, and deep history, it concerns such topics as affect theory, intersensoriality, embodiment, human-animal relations, and distributed cognition.

Cambridge Elements ☰

Histories of Emotions and the Senses

Printed in the United States
By Bookmasters